This is the real-life account of a family who walked through hell on earth. David and Marie are my heroes. The way they dealt with this tragedy is a testimony to the amazing power of God's extraordinary grace, and proves once again that He is with those who love Him, no matter how horrific the circumstances.

If you're like me, you won't be able to put this book down until you've read the final word of the final chapter. It's the inside story of what took place. It's engaging and powerful, and it will rock you to the very core of your soul.

—PETER WARREN
Director of Youth With A Mission (Denver)

When it seems as though this generation is spiraling out of control, the powerful testimony of the Works family in the midst of the tragic loss of their two daughters stands as a reminder that faith endures to the end. David and Marie Works have allowed God's forgiveness, healing, and grace to work a miracle in their family that surpasses any human expectation.

—RON LUCE
President and Founder of Teen Mania Ministries

FOCUS
ON THE FAMILY

GONE
IN A HEARTBEAT

Our Daughters Died . . .
Our Faith Endures

DAVID & MARIE WORKS
with Dean Merrill

Tyndale House Publishers, Inc.
Carol Stream, Illinois

Gone in a Heartbeat
Copyright © 2009 by David and Marie Works
All rights reserved. International copyright secured.

A Focus on the Family book published by
Tyndale House Publishers, Inc., Carol Stream, Illinois 60188

Focus on the Family and the accompanying logo and design are trademarks of Focus on the Family, Colorado Springs, CO 80995.

TYNDALE and Tyndale's quill logo are registered trademarks of Tyndale House Publishers, Inc.

Editor: Kathy Davis
Cover design by: Jacqueline L. Nuñez
Cover photograph of Stephanie and Rachel Works courtesy of the Works family.
Cover photograph of New Life Church and Pikes Peak by Joe Sapulich, © copyright Tyndale House Publishers.
All interior photographs courtesy of the Works family unless otherwise noted.
Cycles of Violence and Snail Model diagrams courtesy of Strategies for Trauma Awareness and Resilience (STAR) Center for Justice and Peacebuilding, Eastern Mennonite University. Used by permission.
The Chronicles of Narnia is a registered trademark of C.S. Lewis Pte. Ltd.

David and Marie Works are represented by the literary agency of WordServe Literary Group (www.wordserveliterary.com), in Highlands Ranch, Colorado.

Library of Congress Cataloging-in-Publication Data
Works, David.
    Gone in a heartbeat : our daughters died—our faith endures / David & Marie Works ; with Dean Merrill.
        p. cm.
    "A Focus on the Family book."
    Includes bibliographical references and index.
    ISBN-13: 978-1-58997-548-4 (alk. paper)
    ISBN-10: 1-58997-548-0 (alk. paper)
    1. Children—Death—Religious aspects—Christianity. 2. Assault and battery—Colorado—Colorado Springs. 3. Christian teenagers—Violence against. 4. Christians—Violence against. 5. Works, Stephanie, d. 2007. 6. Works, Rachel, d. 2007. I. Works, Marie. II. Merrill, Dean. III. Title.
    BV4907.W67 2009
    248.8'660922—dc22
    [B]
                                                    2008046286

Printed in the United States of America
1 2 3 4 5 6 7 8 9 / 15 14 13 12 11 10 09

Contents

Foreword by Jack W. Hayford xi

The Prophecy 1
Three Musketeers 9
Growing Up Fast 19
The Church of Our Dreams 37
One Snowy Sunday 53
Hanging by a Thread 65
What Now? 83
Step by Step 97
Two Roses in the Snow 115
Celebration of Life 127
A Christmas Like No Other 139
Rhythms of Grace 149
Parents in Pain 157
Back to "Normal"? 169
A Platform for Forgiveness 181
Sunshine and Tears 191
What We Know—and Don't Know 201

Afterword by Brady Boyd 211
Appendix 215
Notes 217

Who shall separate us from the love of Christ?
Shall tribulation, or distress, or persecution, or famine,
    or nakedness, or peril, or sword *[or assault rifle]*?
As it is written:

> *"For Your sake we are killed all day long;*
> *We are accounted as sheep for the slaughter."*

Yet in all these things we are more than conquerors
    through Him who loved us.
For I am persuaded that neither death nor life,
    nor angels nor principalities nor powers,
    nor things present nor things to come,
    nor height nor depth, nor any other created thing,
    shall be able to separate us from the love of God
    which is in Christ Jesus our Lord.

—ROMANS 8:35-39 (NKJV)

Foreword

By Jack W. Hayford

The tearful scream and the pounding on the office door were the first shock, but the gunshots immediately following, ringing from the foyer directly below us, announced the emotional and death-dealing earthquake that had already begun in the parking lot outside.

It was Sunday, December 9, 2007—an unforgettable day of death and heartbreak, with that painful pair of realities matched by heroism and divine intervention.

I was there, privileged by Pastor Brady Boyd to be pulpit guest at New Life Church in Colorado Springs that morning, and privileged by God's providence to be a witness to the profound mix of terror, trauma, and transcendent grace.

The pages that follow are a testimony to the horrible being answered by the Holy—of human brokenness and shredding being addressed by divine intervention and mercifulness, at both the instant of shocking impact as well as during the aftermath of the horror. As you read, you will be stirred deeply as well as surprised greatly—just as I was on that day and all the more over the weeks and months that have followed.

Notably, you will gain inspiration and hope as you read and identify with people just like you and me who face sudden fear or instantaneous upheaval. Here is a testimony of how divine peace-amid-storm is available to any of us in such moments.

For example, from the moment the door was opened to Pastor Boyd's assistant, who was desperately crying and beating at the door—

interrupting the quiet postservice lunch we were having—an immediate flow of peace ensued. Her cry was a warning, *"There's a gunman in the building!"* And with that exclamation, I observed a virtual miracle of confidence and wisdom descend over the pastor.

Though Brady is obviously an experienced and wise leader, overseeing a large congregation of well over 10,000, it was moving to me to see transcendent grace overtake a man in a moment of literal "under fire" dimension, as he instantly, with perfect clarity and confidence, began giving instructions and directives to associates in the room. There was no rehearsal or any way to prepare for such a moment; gunfire was being heard downstairs, and there was no way to know the gunman's intended path of pursuit. The stairway was as accessible to the shooter as it was to the assistant who had just arrived. None of us had any reason to doubt our own vulnerability. But unexplainable peace—manifested in instant, decisive, and discerning action—reigned beyond the terror.

To such evidences of God-in-the-middle-with-us examples, you may also be encouraged to believe in the importance of your own simplest words or actions in trying or crisis circumstances. God can and will use any of us in such settings, even when we have no idea what their spiritual impact or blessing may be at the time. Let me illustrate that statement from my personal experience that day.

Swept up in the stunning moments that shook that Sunday, I viewed myself as a mere spectator. Though I had ministered the Word of God to several thousand people during the two services preceding the outbreak of terror, when the lightning moments began to strike, I felt numb rather than afraid and unimportant rather than significant.

Naturally, I joined in prayer with Brady and others in the room— and continued praying as he began to issue directives. I was there with him, available and present to encourage or serve, but I was not a key player in any way. I saw it as a moment to be handled by people familiar with the setting, the staff, the resources, the campus, and what to do then and there. Yet Pastor Boyd would later relate to me—as did others—how strengthened they felt by my presence, how partnered they felt I was with them in the crisis, and how thankful they were for my help.

Please understand—I am not mentioning these things for self-affirming reasons. I write that paragraph to affirm *you*! As you read, I want to urge you to do so with a dual expectancy. The first, obviously, is to expect your faith and hope to be uplifted as you hear David and Marie Works's story; to be astonished by the raw disaster they faced; and then to be more than amazed by the way destructive disaster turned into a divinely directed outcome filled with the comfort and confidence of God's goodness beyond horror.

Second, however, I invite you to place yourself in the moment, because we all face them—indeed, doubtless many who read my words already have. Sudden fear and terrorizing trauma are common intruders into our human situation. God's Word speaks to the reality of "sudden fear," "sudden terror," or "sudden disaster" in Proverbs 3:25-26:

> *Do not be afraid of sudden terror, nor of trouble from the wicked*
> *when it comes; for the LORD will be your confidence, and will keep*
> *your foot from being caught.* (NKJV; see also KJV and NIV)

Whether you are an onlooker, as I was, or one of the principal parties, as were the Works family and Pastor Boyd—God has placed you there to be an instrument, however surprising such a possibility may be to you or me! To conclude, I offer this last example.

It was about 11:30 that morning. The second service was in progress, and I had been resting in the pastor's office to refresh myself before speaking again. None could know that within less than two hours the gunman's onslaught would become a part of the day's history. I was headed back to the sanctuary, and as I briskly moved across the foyer, a slender woman approached with an extended hand—apologizing for her request that I stop a moment. She simply said, "Pastor Hayford, you don't know me, but your ministry has blessed me more than you know. I simply wanted to meet you and shake your hand."

She continued, "I won't be able to hear you this morning because I have a ministry assignment during this service." I affirmed my gratitude, being careful to avoid being hasty and careful to express my appreciation for her faithfulness to the task that required her presence elsewhere in the church. I breathed the simplest of prayers over her, such as, "God bless you, Jeanne," since she had said her name when introducing herself.

Little did I know, *I had just blessed the hand that would fire the gun that would take the shooter down in the church, a little over 100 minutes later!* Jeanne Assam, a member of New Life, was a part of the security team overseeing the church site that morning—a trained and licensed policewoman whose almost dainty size belied the capability, skill, and preparedness that would make her a key part of the day, though her role was entirely other than any she would have wished for.

Indeed, we never know what role we may play in any moment of sudden terror. You will find David and Marie to be victims who became victors through such a moment. I discovered Brady to be a startled pastor who instantly became a confident general in a moment of warfare. And I afterward found myself, a virtual nonentity in that moment, become an actual boon and bestower of blessing in it.

As you read, amid the inspiration you'll find, let me invite you to expect something of an incarnation to take place in your own heart as well. The same Holy Spirit that enabled ordinary people like those herein to deal with a moment of upheaval and loss is ever ready to breathe His same power and wisdom into you—*in a moment.*

Yes, *in a heartbeat.*

—JACK W. HAYFORD
President, International Foursquare Churches
Chancellor, The King's College and Seminary,
Los Angeles, California

THE
PROPHECY

Our twins were ten years old, and our younger daughters were eight and two, when something truly terrible happened in our city. I (Marie) was driving down a Denver avenue that Tuesday morning in our blue Oldsmobile with Laurie sitting across from me, while Stephanie and Rachel were stuffed into the back alongside Gracie in her car seat. We would resume our home-schooling lessons once we returned from these errands to our storage unit and the post office.

The music on the radio suddenly faded out for a news bulletin. I didn't have time to shield my daughters' young ears from the shocking words. "A shooting spree is underway at Columbine High School in Littleton. Authorities are now on the scene trying to contain the damage. It appears there may be more than one shooter at work—there are multiple victims both inside the school and out on the grass. . . . We're not sure at this point how many casualties there may be, or whether there have been any fatalities. Stay tuned for this fast-breaking story, and we'll keep you updated as soon as we get further information."

I wanted to keep listening, but I didn't want to upset my girls. In fact, it was too late. "Mom! Mom! What's going on? What's happening?" the twins and Rachel seemed to chorus all at the same time. Little Gracie was mercifully too young to catch the impact.

I turned off the radio and wondered what I should say. "Something bad is happening at a school across town," I said at last. "It sounds like someone has brought a gun to school and is shooting at people. I don't know why."

"Is anybody going to die?" Stephanie wanted to know, her dark brown hair framing a serious face in my rearview mirror.

"I sure hope not," I replied, trying to be optimistic. "You don't have to be afraid. We're here on the east side, and that school is over on the southwest side."

"Mom, who brought the gun?" asked Laurie.

"Again, I don't know," I answered. "We'll turn on the TV as soon as we get home and find out more." My inquisitive girls, I knew, could not be diverted from this awful event; their curiosity was fully piqued by now. We began to pray aloud in the car. "God, please send Your angels to protect the innocent people," I said. "Please stop this awful thing that's going on."

When we got home, I called my husband, David, who was at his job downtown with USWest, the regional phone company. "Turn on a TV!" I said. "There's a terrible shooting going on at Columbine High School!"

"Yes, I know!" he replied. "We don't have any TVs here in the office, but everybody's got a radio going. There's no work happening around here. It's awful, isn't it!"

For the rest of the day, we thought of little else. We were stunned, like everyone else, at this bolt of unexpected slaughter. We found out that two students, Eric Harris and Dylan Klebold, had come to the campus heavily armed and firing wildly. We saw video footage from a helicopter showing students running away from the building in panic. We saw ambulances screeching toward hospitals with lights flashing and sirens blaring. We heard police spokespeople trying to assure the public that they would soon have the situation under control.

By that evening when David got home from work, the bloody toll was becoming clear: 12 students and one teacher shot to death, the two perpetrators had committed suicide, plus 27 others had been taken to hospitals, some of them in critical condition. Survivors told harrowing tales of hiding in closets and under library tables. Denver radio and TV stations were covering the story nonstop. National media were picking it up as well.

That evening we sat together in the living room talking about the events of the day. We tried to get the facts straight as well as sort out several theories being raised by the news media.

"Daddy," Stephanie asked, "why would someone shoot their classmates?"

"I don't know, honey. I can't imagine a reason for that," David replied. "There's no good reason—other than that there is evil in our world. Evil comes from Satan, and he's out to hurt anyone he can."

David and I finally went to bed pondering what a violent society we had become. Couldn't you even take your children to a public building in a suburban area anymore and assume they would be safe? What dangers lurked in the shadows waiting to pick off innocent kids for no reason? *Oh, God, comfort those parents who are just devastated tonight*, we murmured. *And somehow protect us all.*

CARD FACTORY

The next day, we tried to resume the normal rhythms of home-school. When the spelling and math and social-studies lessons were finished, I noticed 10-year-old Laurie getting out construction paper and markers to make something at the kitchen table. She seemed very intent on her art project, whatever it was.

Her sisters came by before long and said, "Laurie, what are you doing?"

"I'm making cards," she explained.

"For who?" Stephanie and Rachel wanted to know.

"For the kids in the hospital. I'm going to make a get-well card for each one of them." She busied herself with folding and cutting unique shapes. She began decorating them with flowers and smiley faces.

"That's cool!" her sisters responded. "We want to do some too. Can we help?"

Soon all three were busy making works of art for those in the hospital they didn't even know. They weren't sure how many cards to create. I told them that when their dad got home that evening, he could go online and try to find out the names of those who were hurt.

By the next day, a list of patients and their locations had been assembled. It appeared that nearly all were clustered in three large hospitals: University, Swedish, and Denver Health Medical Center.

Laurie wrote each name on a finished card. "Can we take them around to the kids?" she asked with upturned face. "I don't want to just mail them; I want us to deliver them ourselves."

"Well, maybe we could do that on Saturday, when I'm off work," David replied. Naturally, the girls weren't thrilled to have to wait that long, but it was the most realistic plan.

As it turned out, getting to the actual patients was not a simple task, given the fact that the attention of the whole city was on them. More than once we had to leave our card at a nurses' station, hoping it would be delivered the rest of the way down the hall. But sometimes we were able to work our way to the actual bedside. At University Hospital, we accidentally ran into the mother of Mark Taylor at the elevators.

"Excuse me," Laurie said, holding out her creation, "but I made something. This is for your son."

The woman looked blankly at us for a second, then said, "Oh, that's really kind of you. Thank you so much!" We started talking, and soon she began to cry. "There have been more than a few unusual people stopping by, it seems. I just . . . it's so nice that you thought of us," she added, reaching down to give Laurie a pat.

We kept working down the list until all the cards were delivered. Then we turned our car in the direction of Columbine. We wanted to see for ourselves the place where the carnage had broken loose.

When we arrived, the campus was busy with hundreds of other families and individuals just like us. All of Denver and the state was gripped by what had happened there. We got out and began walking around the buildings, noting the broken windows and identifying the parking lots we had seen on television. It was hard to get close because a large area was still marked off with yellow crime-scene tape.

We saw impromptu memorials everywhere. It was clear a lot of people were overcome with emotion. We put our flowers with gold and white ribbons (the school colors of Columbine High) on a long fence by the tennis courts, which seemed to be the biggest memorial wall.

Everywhere we went, it was quiet, like a cathedral. To speak in a loud voice would have seemed irreverent.

A wet snow had fallen, even though this was the third week of April, turning many areas to mud. We slipped and skidded our way up a large hill behind the school. Looking out across the suburban rooftops of quiet Littleton, it was hard to believe this had really happened in a part of our city. But the plywood covering the school windows and the military police in their Humvees could not be denied.

The next afternoon after church, we attempted to go to the public memorial service in Clement Park that had been organized by Colorado's new governor, Bill Owens. Phil Driscoll would play his amazing trumpet, and the two Cohen brothers who had survived the shooting would sing their new song, "Friend of Mine (Columbine)." The main speaker would be Franklin Graham, son of the famous evangelist.

When we got there, the place was so overwhelmed with people we couldn't find a parking spot. We sized up the challenge and decided it would be better to go back home and watch the service on TV.

In the coming weeks, however, we did succeed in attending other memorial events across the city. Our whole family wanted to stay in touch with this tragedy; Laurie had gotten us started with her card-making, and we wanted to stand in support of anyone in pain. We went to a service at the Foursquare church where the Cohen family attended; we also took in a big outdoor concert on Fiddler's Green that featured, among other groups, the Christian band called the Newsboys.

A student ministry called Revival Generation organized a rally at Cherry Hills Community Church, an evangelical megachurch on the south edge of the city. At least 2,000 attended. The keynote speaker, Josh McDowell, spent an hour with us adults in a breakout session. He spoke openly about the issues our society was facing with young people. I also stood at the back of the main auditorium, where the youth session was held. There was fervent prayer, some music by recording artist Wayne Watson, and straight talk.

Through all of these experiences that spring of 1999, we found new appreciation for God's ability to give strength to the wounded and courage to those stricken by unexpected evil. Our entire family learned afresh that the world is not always a nice place. Terrible things happen, and when they do, it's good to lean upon God's arm all the more.

A STRANGE WORD

The capstone of the post-Columbine events for us occurred that August, just before school resumed. An organization called Torchgrab put together another large youth rally to be held in the Ascot Theater in Littleton. The name reflected the call to "pick up the torch" of faith that had been carried by such Columbine victims as Rachel Scott and

Cassie Bernall. Both of them had been strong Christians, much to the irritation of their killers.

Once again, we went as a family. Under each seat was a bag of interesting freebies—a youth devotional book, a music CD, a *Who Is Jesus?* video, some Bible-study materials—that the girls thought was neat. A thousand kids filled the theater that night to hear nationally known youth speakers such as Ron Luce (president of Teen Mania), Eastman Curtis, and Bruce Porter, who had organized the event. Also on the program was Cindy Jacobs, an author and speaker, especially on the subject of intercessory prayer. She is also known for giving prophetic statements from time to time.

In her challenge to the young people that night, Cindy retold the stories of Rachel and Cassie. She declared that following Christ in today's world could be an uphill climb. She said, "In fact, I want to say that some of you young people here tonight will eventually be martyrs for the name of Christ." She then went on to call for dedication and determination no matter the cost.

Her stark prediction stuck in our minds, although our girls seemed not to notice. David told me later that on the way home, he thought to himself, *What was THAT all about? Such a blunt prophecy! Why would she even say such a thing to an audience of teenagers already traumatized by the Columbine shootings? Don't they have enough to worry about as it is?*

We put our sleepy girls to bed that night and hoped their futures would be far less ominous.

THREE
MUSKETEERS

When the small-town doctor had told us we were going to have twins, we weren't upset, or even all that surprised. I (David) was in favor of a large family, and so was Marie—a twin herself. In fact, she and her brother had been the fifth and sixth children in a Nebraska family that eventually topped out at nine kids. The area where we lived at the time—the Flathead Valley of northwest Montana—would be perfect for raising children, with its crisp air, big blue sky, soaring mountains on the horizon, and Glacier National Park less than an hour away.

The abundance of scenic beauty couldn't do much to help the fact that I was making just $6.25 an hour as a shoe salesman in those days. We were embarrassed at the grocery store to be using food stamps. My job did, however, include health benefits, and so when Marie went into the hospital early to fend off contractions that started after she fixed a big Thanksgiving meal, the bill was covered. She came back home to spend eight weeks on bed rest, until Stephanie and Laurie made their appearance on January 28, 1989.

"Just before they gave me the epidural that day," Marie remembers, "they did an X-ray to see how the babies were positioned in the womb. I looked at those shapes on the screen and thought to myself, *Wow— they really are two little people, aren't they!* That was my first time to feel overwhelmed. What a huge weight of responsibility we would bear for those two."

Marie's sister Alesia came out from Nebraska to help us for the first six weeks. Marie tried to nurse the girls but could not keep up with them. We had also said beforehand that we were going to be socially responsible and use cloth diapers. That resolve lasted, oh, a couple of hours, after which we were quite willing to begin adding to the landfill.

By the time summer rolled around, however, we were more on top of the challenge. Our sweet girls captured our hearts, despite the work they required of us. We met neighbors who had twins. We got outside in the warm sunshine and began to relish the joys that only parents know.

Of course, we were celebrities among our friends at the "house church" we attended. People loved holding our babies during the meetings in someone's living room or family room; they would tell us how beautiful the girls were and would assure us we were doing a good job. We were bolstered by this loving reinforcement, a key strength of the house-church approach as far as we were concerned.

We would never have pulled away from Montana had it not been for the need to somehow earn more money. We just couldn't go on using public assistance and accepting a fifty-dollar check from my mother each month. In the fall, we packed up a rental truck and headed back to Denver, the area where I had completed college and worked for several years before Marie and I married. My dad, his wife, and my uncle lived there as well. I signed on with the Manpower agency for temporary jobs, one of which eventually led me into the field of information technology.

By the next summer (1990), when the girls were just nicely walking and saying a few words, we realized that—oops!—another baby was on the way. We hadn't exactly planned it that way. And what if we had another set of *twins*? My dear wife was obsessed with the thought, even when an ultrasound showed only a single fetus. "One is hiding behind the other! I just know it," she would tell me. "I'm gaining the same amount of weight as the first time. My mother had three sets of twins before it was all over."

Her premonition proved false when Rachel entered the world by herself on January 26, 1991—two days before the twins' second birthday. She turned out to be a quiet, easy baby to care for. She was, in fact, a breeze after the intensity of her older sisters' early months. She also distinguished herself by having blue eyes and blondish hair that seemed to stick straight up, all in contrast to Stephanie's and Laurie's dark hair and eyes. We loved her deeply.

THREE-RING CIRCUS

But the lure of Montana still tugged at us strongly. It felt like home in a way that Denver did not. I got in touch with a computer dealer up there and offered to do training classes as well as network installations. He agreed to hire me. I assumed the pay would be equal to what the Denver market was paying for this kind of service.

It wasn't quite that good, but we managed somehow, and the next four years in Montana were among our happiest. The girls were growing, becoming more entertaining all the time (both for us and for each other). We read James Dobson's books to figure out how to raise kids, especially appreciating *The Strong-Willed Child*. We came to realize that Stephanie, the firstborn (by all of sixty seconds!), was the boss, the mother hen, always trying to run the show and make sure her sisters did things right. Laurie was more carefree, the one who wanted to stop during walks and pick flowers or just sit down for a while. Yet, if they wanted to, the twins could be co-conspirators, dreaming up plots to benefit themselves at others' expense.

Rachel turned out to be the artistic one of the three. From an early age she was known for creating new ways to dress, putting one dress over another, for example—and making it look nice. One afternoon when she was supposed to be taking a nap, she opted for something more fun. She got water from the bathroom, poured it onto the bedroom carpet, and began stomping and splashing it everywhere. Her explanation to her upset mother? "I'm making a carpet soufflé!"

The three musketeers showed their spunk a bit later by organizing an impromptu trick-or-treat foray when a neighbor's granddaughter happened to be visiting—only it wasn't Halloween. It was, in fact, just after Easter. The foursome figured out that most homes would have leftover Easter candy lying around, so why not knock on their doors and ask for some? They came home with an impressive bag of goodies. Apparently people thought the little girls were too cute to dismiss on the grounds of calendar technicalities. Marie and I were taken aback, but we also had to salute their inventiveness.

We always did a lot of singing in our house. The girls would cluster around Mom when she played the synthesizer. They loved the Maranatha! Praise and Integrity Music tunes that were popular for kids at the time. They would dance and clap with jubilance.

One song that struck their fancy was "Mighty Warrior" by Debbye Graafsma, a good-versus-evil melody with a strong beat. The girls would do their own karaoke version, using the hearth as their stage. The high point was jumping off onto the floor when they reached the line about "crush the enemy!" The big boom of six little feet hitting the floor at once made them shiver with delight. (It also eventually jarred loose a downstairs light fixture directly below the hearth, which I hurried to fix before the landlord came around.)

When we went to our house-church group on Sundays, the girls would sit on the floor in the middle of the circle with the other kids. Sometimes one of them would even suggest a song to be sung, which was typical of this informal atmosphere. On ordinary weekdays, we would sometimes catch our girls playing "church" on the steps down to the basement. One would be the preacher, while the other two would dutifully sit and listen.

We also went on some Friday nights to a nearby training center for young missionaries, operated by a group called Youth with a Mission (YWAM). Their Friday-night meetings were open to the public, and we enjoyed the enthusiasm of worshiping with these eager young people.

It is not surprising, then, that each of the girls came to a point of personal faith during these Montana years. Laurie was the first, at age four. We were having a discussion one night when she asked, "Is God right here? Can He just walk through the door?"

I was caught a bit off guard, but I answered, "Well, yes—of course. God isn't just far away. He's right here with us all the time."

"Really? You mean He could walk right through the door without opening it, or come right through the wall?"

"Yes."

"Daddy. I'm not sure about that," she challenged me. "You mean He's like a ghost or something?"

I decided it might be better to continue this discussion with just the two of us. I took her back to our bedroom, where we sat on the edge of the bed. I asked her what was really troubling her.

She wouldn't answer directly. "Daddy, if God is right here," she said, "then why doesn't He show up? There are so many things that need fixing."

"What are you really saying, honey?"

"It seems to me that if God doesn't do it, I just have to do it myself!"

In that moment, I had a flashback to someone else who had said virtually the same thing several years before. That someone else was me!

"Honey, God can fix those things for you. You don't have to do them yourself. But He's not going to do them for you if you don't make room for Him."

I then continued, "Do you want God to be here right now?"

"Yes, Daddy."

"He will not only show up, but He can come and live inside you. Would you like that?" I was taking a huge chance, I knew. If she said yes, she would really need to experience something. This couldn't just be an intellectual discussion.

"Daddy, would that really happen?"

"Honey, God will never fail you. If you pray along with me, God promises He will show up." By now she was sitting on my lap. We bowed our heads and prayed together that Jesus would welcome her as His child. It was a simple moment, but in our opinion, a significant one. It signaled that she wanted to be a follower of Jesus herself, not just part of the family culture.

We finished our prayer, and when we looked up, we both had a tangible sense that God was there in the room with us. Laurie's face was beaming. "Daddy, I've never felt anything like this!" she exuded. "This is so neat!"

When Stephanie heard what Laurie had done, she wanted to do the same. We pressed her a bit to see if this was just a copycat request. In the end, we were convinced that it represented her genuine desire.

Rachel followed in the same trail not long afterward. We eventually had all three of them baptized in a cold Canadian creek just across the border from where we lived. It was an important marker in their spiritual journey.

Not that any of this turned them into little saints, you understand. They could still be feisty kids in need of parental guidance and correction. They could still squabble with each other over toys or show a rebellious streak now and again. But their hearts were given to Jesus and to trying to do what would please Him.

HOME-SCHOOLING BY ACCIDENT

Our town had a Christian school, and Marie and I intended to send our girls there. But as the enrollment deadline approached to start the twins in prekindergarten, we failed to pay attention. Suddenly we learned that paperwork needed to be submitted, along with a sizable tuition down payment. We weren't prepared. Now what?

Stephanie and Laurie had a ready alternative to suggest. "We really want to learn to read," they chorused. "So, Daddy, if we can't go to that school, then *you* have to teach us!"

Well, maybe home-schooling would be an option for us. We knew that several other families in our house church were doing this. We began to ask questions and gather information. We got a copy of *The Big Book of Home Learning* by Mary Pride, which was the home-schooling authority of that time, and dove in. Soon Marie was doing actual lessons with the girls at their small play table. We started down the home-education road almost by accident.

The twins proved to be quick learners, as was Rachel when she started a couple of years later. Both mother and daughters were stimulated by the process. I jumped in to help with math when I could.

And in the back of our minds, this approach dovetailed with a larger goal for our family that Marie and I often talked about. We didn't believe God wanted us simply to be the typical American family raising kids and chasing the good life. My long-term dream was not to build a comfortable career in information technology. We held a sense of calling to a special mission.

It traced back to an unusual moment in my life, about three months after I had become an intentional Christian at the age of 28. I was still single at the time, and on this particular Sunday morning, I was sitting in a class at Denver's Calvary Temple. The teacher, one of the church's associate pastors, began the class with a song or two, then invited us all to bow our heads for prayer.

I closed my eyes along with the other 50 people in the rows and, without warning, found myself still seeing images. I was engulfed in a different reality; the sounds of the classroom faded out. I found myself in a surreal encounter with Jesus Christ.

If I told you all the details of the vision that ensued over the next few minutes, you might scoff. I can offer no tangible record, no video-tape of what I saw and heard. I can only tell you it was incredibly real. I was swept up in the experience, which reached its pinnacle with these divine words: "If you put Me in a small box, I will work within it. If you put Me in a larger box, I will work in it. But if you give Me everything, I will give you everything. I have called you to be a witness of things you have seen, are seeing, and will yet see. Receive!"

Immediately I saw a globe turning slowly. It started from the West Coast of the United States, rotated out across the Pacific, and came to East Asia, then Central Asia, and on toward Africa and Europe. As it did, five cities lit up with a glowing red light: Beijing (China), Bangkok (Thailand), a city in northern India that I later identified as Varanasi, then Nairobi (Kenya), and finally, Lagos (Nigeria). I had the distinct impression that I would someday go to these places to do some kind of work for God.

And then the vision faded. I was still in my seat in the church class-room and was shocked to hear the teacher just concluding his prayer, ". . . in Jesus' name, amen." I felt as if an hour had passed, but apparently it had been only minutes.

I sat shaken with emotion. I glanced around, expecting the whole room of people to be staring at me. However, nobody looked my way. The class proceeded in normal fashion.

Again, I admit that you may dismiss this phenomenon as the product of an overwrought mind, a young man dreaming up crazy fantasies, even a flare of mental instability. I choose to believe that God was indeed communicating with me in the same way He spoke to people in Bible times—Ezekiel, Daniel, Zechariah the aged priest, Cornelius the Roman centurion, Peter on the rooftop, and others. I, like they, didn't fully know what it meant. I only felt the power of its impact.

After I met Marie a year later, I waited for the right circumstance to tell her about this unusual event. She didn't dismiss me as a crackpot. Rather, she accepted the vision as an indicator of what our future life together would entail—though neither one of us could say when or how.

Now, nine years later in Montana with three growing girls, we said to each other, "Well, if the Lord is going to send us around the world someday as a missionary family, maybe it's good that we're already home-schooling. That would make travel a lot easier, wouldn't it? Maybe this is another piece of the puzzle. Who can say for sure?"

There were no signs at the time that anything dramatic was going to change in our day-to-day lives. I kept going to work each day, paying the bills, and doing with Marie what normal parents do. We laughed through the good times and prayed our way through the challenges, trusting that God would roll out His larger strategy for us whenever He saw fit.

GROWING UP
FAST

Long-term hopes and dreams were all fine, but in the meantime, another baby was on the way. We looked at our present income, calculated the cost of becoming a family of *six*, and talked about what we might do to increase the cash flow. What about getting back into sales, a field where David had been successful in the past?

He began exploring his options and in time landed a sales job with a computer training company back in Denver. That meant moving again—and the sooner the better, before the pregnancy got too far along. So in May 1996, we once again loaded up the Ryder rental truck and struck out on the long road from Whitefish, Montana, to the Colorado capital—a thousand miles away.

Stephanie, then seven and a half, was sad to leave behind a close friend named Carly. When we arrived, however, she was easily distracted by our family's adventure of spending the first six weeks up at Gramps Works's rustic cabin in Gilpin County, an hour's drive west of Denver. There, at an altitude of 9,000 feet, we relished the tall trees and mountain meadows full of wildflowers, while David commuted into the city each day for his job.

Ground squirrels and rabbits were everywhere. So were the white-tailed deer. At night we could hear coyotes howling. Five-year-old Rachel came running back to the cabin in a panic one day insisting she had seen a bear down by the pond. She was right, because later on, her grandfather got a picture of one in the meadow.

By midsummer, a house-church friend we had known in the past offered us the use of a town house in the suburb of Parker. We knew this wouldn't be permanent, but at least it would shorten David's travel time. Soon after the move, our girls got to know children in the new neighborhood. One day Stephanie came in all excited, followed by her two sisters.

"Mom, guess what? Amanda just became a Christian! It was so cool!"

"Really? That's great!" I (Marie) responded. "Tell me all about it."

She launched into a description, with her sisters adding detail along the way. Several days later, the story repeated itself with more of their friends.

"We have to get Bibles for them," they insisted. "Can we go buy some? Please?" I readily agreed. Our daughters were catching the missionary spirit already.

The Fourth of July was a big thing at our house, that year and every year. David has always had a love affair with fireworks. He and his brother grew up setting off cherry bombs and M-80s in their yard back in Kansas City. In Montana, he had gotten the girls interested in smoke bombs, "artillery shells" (sky rockets), and other explosives you could buy on the Indian reservations. Laurie and Rachel were the most curious; I jokingly accused my husband of trying to turn them into little "pyros" just like him.

Colorado turned out to have stricter laws on all this (much to my relief). You couldn't set off anything that left the ground. "What a drag," David moaned as he began researching nearby areas, such as Wyoming, that might be a bit more lenient.

A different kind of fizzle was occurring, unfortunately, in the workplace. Sales successes were few and far between, not only for David but also for the company's other reps. The market seemed to have shifted, and nobody could quite figure out why or in what direction. By early fall, his job collapsed. And our baby was due around Thanksgiving. What now?

We seriously talked about going back to Montana. "But is that really what the Lord has in mind?" one of us said to the other. "Maybe we came here as just the first step toward our greater mission. Maybe we'll soon be heading out for parts unknown." We decided to sit tight in Denver.

David returned to the tech side of his talents, lining up a contract job supporting a computer network at a hospital. This would carry us through the first of the year. We found a pair of midwives who would deliver the baby at home, thereby saving costs. On the Saturday after Thanksgiving, contractions began, and we called them to come.

The baby, however, was in the breech position. After several hours of struggle, we ended up racing down the highway to University Hospital. David honestly thought we weren't going to make it. I spent the time praying.

The actual delivery that day was hard, involving forceps. But in the end, God gave us another healthy little girl weighing seven pounds. We named her Grace Emily. When we brought her home 24 hours later, her three older sisters were ecstatic. We felt relieved that all had ended well.

SQUEEZED

Once the euphoria subsided, we began to find that the combination of a new baby and a shaky job could be stressful. On top of those concerns, we were also wondering about our home-church situation. For more than a decade, David and I had championed this form of Christian worship and community; we had said it was authentic, warm, and biblical, as well as relaxed. It appealed to both of us after our difficulties growing up in formal churches. But now, we had to admit that the house-church scene could be awfully disorganized, almost chaotic at times. Nobody had the authority to structure anything. Our girls were getting old enough to benefit from specialized youth programs, of which there were none. Our house-church network also lacked the structure to guide people like us into overseas ministry.

David went one Sunday to a large, multiracial church in Denver to hear a guest speaker he had known. He came home excited about the experience, so that the rest of us went back with him the next week. We enjoyed the lively music, and we appreciated the preaching as well. Sometime in January after David's hospital project ended, he volunteered to help the church office with some networking problems. Soon they wanted to hire him to manage this area. This, we decided, would become our church home as well as our livelihood.

It would have been tacky to keep staying in the house-church friend's town house for free, so we found an inexpensive three-bedroom apartment near the church in a complex that included a fair number of low-income subsidized tenants. But we were going to food banks ourselves, so we fit right in.

At 900 square feet, it was a tight fit for the six of us. The twins shared one bedroom, with bunk beds, while Rachel and baby Grace shared another. David taught us a motto using a word he had learned during his early years in the cuckoo-clock business before we were married: "Keep track of your own *Gelumpe!*" (which is Black Forest German dialect for "junk"). It became a family proverb tossed back and forth whenever anyone couldn't find a shoe, an important paper, a hairbrush, or other personal belonging.

I have to admit that with a newborn, I wasn't the most effective home-school teacher that year. At times I felt truly overwhelmed. The cramped quarters and the difficulty of daily living with just one car took their toll. Plus, we lived with the expectation that we might be moving again soon. As a result, we didn't really settle in. We kept things in a storage unit. We didn't hang pictures on the walls for several years.

I didn't talk a lot about my emotional state, however. That had never been my style. The truth is, I've always been a quiet person. Some of that may have to do with a traumatic period in my early childhood, when it seemed that my feelings were swept aside in the aftermath of a tragedy. My mother had gone to the basement of our Nebraska farmhouse one day to relight the water heater's pilot flame, which had gone out. She didn't realize that gas had already been escaping into the room. The instant she lit the match, there was a huge explosion. The entire house shook, windows were blown out, and she was horribly burned, with second- and third-degree burns over 85 percent of her body.

My father was away at work. My older brother Dan and sister Becky had been watching TV. They told me to run to the barn and get my other brothers and sisters. By the time I got back, my mother was lying on her bed in agony. I remember kneeling beside her there and crying, "Where's my daddy? If only my daddy were here, everything would be okay!"

She spent months recuperating in the hospital, and meanwhile, we eight kids were parceled out to various relatives and friends. I ended up being sent with my two oldest brothers to stay with some people who seemed not all that excited to have us. I didn't even get to retain the special link with my twin, Mark. *Nobody cares how I feel about this*, I realized. *Nobody asks what I'm thinking*.

From there, it was but a short step for me to conclude that nobody needed to know how I felt. Why bother trying to tell them? In fact, in subsequent years I wasn't entirely sure how I felt about things myself. I had seriously disconnected from my emotional side.

Later on, when I became a Christian, I was restored to a heavenly Father who would always be at my side. This was a great comfort. But my pattern of shutting off my feelings and detaching from any expression of anxiety, fear, or frustration remained ingrained in my personality. Better to just keep quiet, I told myself.

YOUTHFUL ENERGY

Our girls, on the other hand, seemed oblivious to my suppressed way of dealing with life. David and I are amazed, as we look back now, at how well our girls adapted to our bumpy circumstances. When Denver got hit with a blizzard, they would race outside to make snow angels and forts for snowball fights in the parking lot. They all seemed to love winter—perhaps because, in addition to Christmas, it was birthday season for all four of them. We got them individual library cards and became avid patrons, checking out stacks of books nearly every week all through the coming years.

The girls were always thinking of ways to make money so they could go places and do things. One summer day they said, "Hey, Mom, it's really hot outside. We want to set up a lemonade stand in the parking lot. Will you help us?" Soon they were hawking cool drinks to all the neighbors. They didn't just sit down and wait for business; they were serious businesswomen up on their feet calling attention to their product. Over a three-day period they brought in $75. Soon the other kids in the complex began competing with them, so the proceeds were not as fat.

As the girls got older, David took them fly-fishing up in the mountains. (Anything to escape the apartment.) They loved wading into the cold stream to cast. We didn't have money for them to join organized sports teams, but we could still get out in the Colorado wilderness and have a good time. We kept going back up to Gramps's cabin, where we did lots of hiking. The girls built a "clubhouse" of sorts out in the woods—actually, a collection of branches arranged into various "rooms." They named it "Gnadenau Settlement," after the first community set up in central Kansas back in 1874 by Krimmer Mennonite Brethren, who had come from Russia. The girls had read all about it in books and wanted to re-enact the scene. (*Gnade* in German means "grace." Hence, *Gnadenau* equals "meadow of grace.")

On Friday nights, we would go to Channel 41 to join the studio audience of a live Christian TV show called *Celebration*. The mid-1990s were a time of spiritual revival in the Denver area, and this show featured music, personal interviews, and teaching segments by various pastors and speakers. Viewers were even able to call in and receive prayer from counselors at a phone bank. We enjoyed the atmosphere of spiritual expectancy. To us, this was a way of letting God know we wanted to be part of whatever He was doing in the world.

MUDDLING THROUGH

After a year and a half at the church job, David found an opening at USWest for twice the pay. It was 1998 and we had now been married for 11 years, struggling from one wobbly situation to another. With this large telecommunications firm, maybe we could finally start whittling down our debts—especially with the expensive teen years just around the corner. We both were excited.

We put some of our new dollars into the gas tank for Sunday trips up to a revival-minded church in Granby, Colorado, right outside Rocky Mountain National Park. It was much smaller than the megachurch where David had worked, and thus easier for us, with our house-church background, to fit in. Over the next eight years, we came to love the pastor and people there. The two-hour commute each way didn't seem to bother us at all. It felt almost like a weekly getaway to a Montana atmosphere again. Our girls would spend the travel time playing games, singing along with a CD, sleeping, or talking with us about what God might be planning for our family's future.

We also managed a couple of real vacations back to Whitefish in the summer to see old friends. Once we took the girls up on the gondola that the skiers use. From the top, you get a fantastic view of Glacier National Park.

Additionally, David was able to make trips back to Virginia for the annual gathering at Monticello, home of Thomas Jefferson; he's a seventh-generation descendant. Starting in 1999, controversy broke out over DNA research into whether our esteemed third president had also fathered offspring with his slave Sally Hemings. David was on the side of those who believed the reports and therefore accepted their black cousins—much to the irritation of others in the clan. He ended up being quoted and even pictured in such national media as the *New York Times* and *Newsweek* magazine. Our girls thought their dad had become truly famous!

In the winter, we started a Christmas tradition with David's dad and his wife. We would get all dressed up and go for high tea at downtown Denver's historic Brown Palace Hotel. The girls reveled in the elegance, imagining themselves in the same vein as Anne of Green Gables or some character in the Victorian novels they were reading.

Gramps had never bought into the Mormonism of his first wife; in fact, it is fair to say that this was one irritant that led to their divorce back in the early 1980s. He remained an Episcopalian, and on Christmas Day, we would go with him to St. John's Cathedral, even accompanying him up to the high altar to receive the Eucharist. Our girls were intrigued with the symbolism and asked many questions about the liturgy. It was a very reverent experience for us all each year.

Following the service, we would then go to Gramps's genteel home on Marion Street for clam chowder, followed by presents. The day created special memories for us all. (It helped that David and his father were on the same side in the Jefferson debate; David's brother, John Jr., saw things differently.)

And then . . . it was back to the crowded apartment. "Lord, can't we get a house?" I would pray over and over. David and I would review our finances, decide to start looking for a place to buy, but then be disappointed by what the market had to offer. One house after another was close but not quite right for our family. We couldn't understand why the pieces of the puzzle never seemed to fit.

Did this mean that God was getting ready to open a different door for us? Maybe the ministry vision was about to blossom. We didn't know. We tried to be patient and wait for His timing.

After two years at USWest, the company was bought out by an even larger phone giant, Qwest Communications—and David's contract was eliminated along with hundreds of others. Ah-ha! So *this* was the cause of the holdup, we concluded. But nothing developed on the ministry horizon. When an opportunity came in June 2001 to work for First Data Corporation, a financial services company, David went ahead and accepted. We needed to keep buying groceries, right?

The unsettledness in our spirits no doubt had some connection to the drift that seemed to settle in on the home-schooling front. We admit we didn't do the most thorough job as the girls moved into the intermediate grades. We signed them up for an online curriculum from a Christian publisher and assumed this would cover the bases. They did their lessons at the computer for five years.

Eventually we realized they were getting the same material over and over. Boredom began to set in. Motivation lagged. While the twins would keep each other going, Rachel seemed to sag. She never complained about schoolwork, but we saw her continually falling behind in her lessons.

Math was a particular struggle. The girls kept saying, "We don't get it," and David lacked the time to tutor them in this area. We felt isolated, not knowing how to turn things around. We didn't want to nag the girls, sensing inside that the situation was as much our fault as theirs. It was a season of time, educationally speaking, that we now regret.

SPREADING THEIR WINGS

Fortunately, our home-schooling shortcomings never soured their relationship with us as their parents—or their relationship with God. What we lacked in wisdom was apparently offset by passion to pursue God's plan for our life together. As Stephanie and Laurie moved into their teen years, they began to dream about what roles they personally might play.

On May 7, 2003, Stephanie (then 14) wrote in her journal:

> Ever feel like you want to do something so big that it's beyond you? Something so big it makes you excited and about ready to burst? But then you don't know what it is! You want to do something, but you don't know what . . . but just that it has to be big? That's how I feel sometimes. I don't really know . . . yes, I do. The key to finding it is prayer for wisdom.
>
> I read a book about [Columbine victim] Rachel Scott's life yesterday. She didn't know she was going to die. It was sometimes chilling to read her saying she would give all to serve God, because I know in the end she did.

It was very chilling to read that she knew something was up. She had been writing foreboding things and she didn't feel sad. . . .

This drive to make a major difference in the world became a trademark of Stephanie's. She wanted to be a change agent.

In social settings, she wasn't shy about giving compliments to complete strangers. She would walk up to someone and say, "I like your dress—it fits you really well" or "I like the way you did your hair." She loved encouraging people and had a way of doing it without ulterior motives; it was very refreshing.

She also had a curious mind and constantly sought knowledge. For example, she became a connoisseur of exotic teas. She could tell you all kinds of intricate facts about various brands from all over the world. She noticed details. If you watched a historical movie with her—Jane Austen's *Pride and Prejudice*, for example—she would sit there and tell you which piece of costuming wasn't quite right for the period. She had a far-ranging curiosity about many topics.

David heard about these things on his Thursday night "Daddy dates," which got rolling around this time. Each week he would take one of us out to eat, rotating through the family over a five-week cycle. "Where would you like to go tonight?" he would ask, and the girls especially preferred to try someplace new, not the well-worn favorites.

One week Stephanie and David discovered an obscure place on Sixth Avenue near Washington Street called Angelo's Pizza. It didn't look like much from the street, but once they got inside, it had a warm neighborhood feel and great food. The décor almost looked as if the place had once been a church, with stained-glass windows. We went back there as a whole family several times.

On these Daddy-date occasions, the girls could talk about anything on their minds. We found out that the twins, though they loved each other dearly, didn't see eye to eye on everything in life. Laurie's musical tastes tended toward rock, whereas Stephanie was a classical buff. It got to one point, in fact, where the two of them said, "Let's switch room-mates. We're too different on too many things!" So Laurie moved in with Rachel (and all her stuffed animals), while Stephanie and little Grace shared a room.

Rachel, the artistic one, expressed her creativity in manifold ways. She wasn't the "kid sister" in the shadow of older siblings by any means. One day she announced to the twins, "Guess what? I've shaved my arms!"

"You did *what?!*" Stephanie and Laurie shot back. "That's crazy! Why would you do a thing like that?"

"I just felt like it," Rachel said, not really answering the question. "I don't care if you guys approve or not." She simply wanted to express herself.

But more important than fashion statements or music choices was the girls' heart to do something notable for God. Not just someday when they were fully adult, but now. They found out that the youth organization called Teen Mania was sponsoring short mission trips (one or two weeks long) for kids their age. They got very excited about one trip in particular, an outreach to Panama to serve children in poverty and share the gospel with them.

Of course, it meant coming up with a couple of thousand dollars each. They turned to their grandfather as a possible donor.

"Gramps, we really want to go on this work trip to Panama this sum-mer," they pleaded. "Do you think you could help us with a donation?"

"Well, tell me about it," he replied. "Who's running this thing? When would you be going? How are they going to keep you all in line? What about saving this money for college?" Gramps could be a tough customer when he wanted to be.

The girls answered his questions as best they could. They also told him they were gearing up for a bake sale outside the nearby Wal-Mart to help raise money. "Will you come and buy stuff from us, please?"

"Okay, I can do that much," he answered with a smile. In the back of his mind (he told us later), he wasn't all that thrilled with the concept; it brought back memories of his own son's excursion to Europe long ago as a Mormon missionary. But at least he would show up and buy a cake or two from his granddaughters.

A Major Loss

In the end, the girls' dream did not come to pass; our family simply didn't have a large enough network of contacts to raise the necessary funds. As for Gramps, he had his own worries to attend to. By September 2003 it was becoming clear that something was wrong internally. He seemed to be losing weight, and his color didn't look healthy.

The doctor's diagnosis stunned us all: cancer of the bile duct. Surgery was called for, although the survival odds were no better than 50 percent, he said. Gramps took a dim view of that prospect and opted to wait and see. He elected to avoid the monthly checkups the doctor had requested.

By Thanksgiving dinner that year, the whole family could see he was in trouble. We insisted he go back to the doctor again. Throughout the Christmas season, we could see Gramps growing weaker, and by January he landed in the intensive-care unit with a full-blown sepsis infection.

When we took the girls to see him, they were shocked. Here the man who had led them on hikes in the high mountains was now lying barely conscious. As soon as we retreated from the ICU, they burst into tears. "Is Gramps going to die?" they sobbed.

"Well, it looks like it," David had to admit. "The doctors say he might have just a week to live."

But then, stents were inserted into his duct, and to everyone's surprise, the 78-year-old patriarch rallied. He strengthened to the point of being able to transfer to a care facility for a week of recuperation, and he was back in his own home in time to watch the Super Bowl with us on February 1. The girls were thrilled to have their Gramps back again.

His health tracked up and down and back up again throughout the rest of the winter. In early March, he landed back in the hospital with another sepsis outbreak. In the medical briefings we began hearing the word *terminal*. The cancer was going to prevail at last, it seemed.

One day the girls raised a new question on their minds: "Is he going to heaven?"

"Yes," we assured them, "Gramps really has made his peace with God. He's done it within his own tradition, which is more formal than ours. But he does have a very deep spiritual relationship with God. Before you were born, he and his wife even went on retreats with Bishop Frey up near Granby."

We kept watching his deterioration week by week, and it was tough for us all. He moved into a well-managed hospice. Rachel, then 13, admitted in her journal that she wished her beloved Gramps could escape his misery . . . but then she quickly added that she felt guilty for wanting him to die. She was caught, along with us all, in that twilight where there are no easy answers.

On Saturday night, May 1, 2004, we all went to the hospice to see Gramps once again. He was no longer communicative. But we played a video of his favorite movie anyway, *The African Queen*, with Humphrey Bogart and Katharine Hepburn. In the middle of things, he surprised us by starting to talk! His words were mostly unintelligible. But we knew he was connecting with us on at least a simple level, and it gave us comfort.

We left around 11 o'clock that evening, planning to return the next day. At 6:45 on Sunday morning, however, the hospice nurse called to say Gramps was gone. It was our 17th wedding anniversary. In a somber sort of way, we felt honored that he had finalized his earthly journey on our day. We gathered our girls around us and gave thanks together for his life. We held his memorial service at St. John's, followed by a gathering at his beloved cabin in the mountains.

ON THE GO

Our growing girls kept making the best of their crowded circumstances as summer arrived. Their creativity found an outlet the next year (2005) when Denver's famous Tattered Cover bookstore announced a short-story contest. The girls got busy writing. Stephanie won second place in the 9th-10th grade division with a piece called "Wild Thing" about a girl on a Texas ranch with lots of brothers who decides to break a horse herself. The whole setting tells you something about Stephanie: it's full of dust and drama and fearlessly taking on a big challenge. (In fact, as of this writing, the Tattered Cover Web site still carries a link to the story text.[1])

The next year, Rachel produced a very different kind of piece, in keeping with her personality. "Water Fairy" describes a distraught young girl named Emma who runs through the forest to a stream, where fanciful things happen, including the arrival of a handsome male fairy "with shoulder-length light brown hair, a silky blue shirt, and shimmering black pants." The happy ending is pure delight. This story placed high in the contest as well.

In a Nancy Rue novel for girls titled *Lily's in London*, Rachel read about the practice of praying before a lit candle as a way of focusing one's attention. She got a collection of candles for her room—some large, some small, some tall, some short—and began using them during her devotion times. She wasn't trying to overhaul our customs or anything; she simply wanted to experiment with a fresh approach to prayer.

The rest of us thought it was novel but appropriate. We eventually set up a collection of candles on a table where we all could enjoy them from time to time. This was in addition to our normal practice of impromptu prayer, which could happen anytime. We wanted prayer to be a lifestyle in our family.

Sometimes prayer involved the spiritual discipline of fasting as well. We didn't impose it on the kids; we simply explained what the Bible said and then left it up to them to participate with the two of us, or not. We found the experience to be enriching and invigorating as we sought to know God better.

Rachel was the first to actually have a short-term missions experience, even though she was only 14 years old. It took some research on our part to be assured that Teen Mania really could manage a group that young. We read the material carefully and checked out the logistics of the trip to make sure adequate precautions were in place. In the end, we couldn't say no to a daughter eager to serve the Lord. Our portion of Gramps's estate money had recently come our way, and so we had the funds to make this possible.

On the month-long trip to Brazil, Rachel had an amazing time. She also got sick with an intestinal bug of some kind, enough to be hospitalized briefly. Even that served to stretch her coping skills. When she came home at last with glowing reports of how the ministry had gone, she seemed two years older.

That same summer, Stephanie and Laurie went to a one-week camp on a college campus called Worldview Academy. It taught about different religions and how to respond to them from a biblical point of view.

A year later (2006), the twins finished their high-school studies. They took the GED test to qualify for an official diploma, and passed with flying colors. Our shortcomings along their educational trail didn't seem to show at the finish line after all. We were relieved.

The idea of more mission trips captured the girls' imaginations.

Maybe the Works family wasn't going overseas all together at the same time to serve God, as we had long dreamed. But in bits and pieces, we were making a contribution. We were giving God a bigger and bigger box in which to work. David and I looked at our growing daughters, and despite all our missteps, we felt proud.

THE CHURCH
OF OUR DREAMS

When the beloved pastor of our church up in the mountains resigned, and the congregation seemed to be heading in a different direction, we really had to ask ourselves if we should keep making this long trek every Sunday. Our older girls were teenagers now, and the chance to be involved in youth activities was hard to arrange. One round trip a week over Berthoud Pass (11,307 feet) was about all we could handle.

We had of course heard of the huge New Life Church on the north edge of Colorado Springs, the largest congregation in the whole Rocky Mountain region, with some 14,000 attending. We had visited there for various conferences and concerts over the years. In fact, I (David) had been in touch all the way back to 1997, when I was working for the church in Denver and had driven down to investigate New Life's projection software for displaying song lyrics on big overhead screens.

The route from our apartment to the New Life campus was "only" 55 miles on fairly level interstate highways—a breeze compared to the distance we'd been driving for so long. Our three older girls attended the church's summer internship for teens called DSI (Desperation Summer Intensive) and came home raving about how great it was. The deep connection with God, the high-energy music, the straight-talk teaching, the service opportunities, the numerous new friends—everything made the girls coax us in this direction.

By September 2006, we were pretty much regular attenders on Sunday mornings. We relished the sense of God's presence in the joyful praise, the times of fervent prayer, and the passionate preaching. New Life is not a church where you have to work to stay awake. As soon as the band begins the first song of the morning, the spotlights come alive, and young people come out of their seats to swarm the front. There they clap, raise their hands, and even dance in jubilant worship before the Lord. Our girls were right in the thick of it.

Stephanie and Laurie, having completed high school by now, wanted to attend the Friday-night meetings of theMILL (yes, that's the official way to write the name), a group of up to a thousand college-age people. We began accommodating this drive as well. We'd never seen our daughters so happy, making new friends and growing in their personal faith. The crowd was large enough that no one cared about a few parents (like me or Marie) hanging around the back of the auditorium where they met. We enjoyed the meetings as much as the kids.

Laurie quickly found a guy she was interested in, and she began nudging her twin to do the same. Stephanie had always been reluctant in this area, even though she was certainly attractive. We had talked in our family over the years about not needing to be aggressive or follow the norms of a boy-crazy culture, but rather to seek the kind of young man who would please God. The girls had, in fact, read Joshua Harris's best-seller *I Kissed Dating Goodbye*[2] and agreed with the author's viewpoint. We weren't legalistic about this, but we did want them to avoid the traps of premature involvement.

I had to admit, however, that theMILL was a pretty good place for my daughters to test the waters. The goal of finding a godly young man for the future could certainly be pursued there. It was definitely preferable to the apartment complex where we lived, which by this time had seriously deteriorated. Drug dealers were living in some of the units, we were sure. Parties ran loudly into the early morning hours. Domestic arguments between husbands and wives, and teens and their parents, echoed through the thin walls. The police had to be called nearly every weekend.

For our family, New Life Church became a haven. We would linger after services as long as we could, talking with fellow worshipers or praying with a staff pastor. We felt safe there, away from the rancor and hostility of the apartment complex, which was becoming more oppressive all the time. Even the girls were showing frustration. Back when they were little, they had seemed oblivious to our humble quarters. But as they grew older and more aware, they felt the squeeze as well as the turbulence. They began expressing their unhappiness. Sundays were a welcome getaway from all this.

By the end of October I felt the distinct impression that New Life could be our home church, even if we went elsewhere in the world for ministry purposes. I shared this with the family during one of our late-evening chats. Everyone was delighted. We agreed together that New Life Church was the answer for us. We would buy into it emotionally, spiritually, and financially. This place was meant for us, and we for it.

BOMBSHELL

Less than 48 hours later, we—along with the entire congregation—got the jolt of our lives. On a radio talk show, a male "escort" in Denver named Mike Jones claimed that New Life's founder and senior pastor, Ted Haggard, had been one of his clients for three years. Jones had provided repeated sexual services, he said, and had also seen Haggard use methamphetamines.

No way. That was ridiculous. There couldn't be any truth to this outlandish statement.

I quickly surmised that, with the midterm election coming up the following Tuesday, this was a clumsy, last-minute attempt to influence the vote on Colorado's Referendum I (allowing domestic partnerships for same-sex couples) and Amendment 43 (reinforcing traditional marriage). If the gay and lesbian community could smear one of the state's most outspoken defenders of biblical morality, maybe more voters would consider their point of view.

When I first mentioned to Stephanie what was being said about the pastor whom she, and the rest of us, so admired, her reaction was "Oh, yeah, right—that's impossible." I fully agreed with her, having watched Ted Haggard's initial response to reporters, in which he denied everything. He was standing in front of his house at night, and his words sounded reasonable. This was the Ted Haggard I was used to hearing from the pulpit.

But then, a day later came the second interview, when reporters caught him at the end of the driveway with his wife and kids in their SUV. He claimed, among other things, that he had acquired the drugs but then thought better of it and decided not to use them.

My heart sank. *Something's wrong here*, I told myself. I went to 9NEWS.com, which had both interviews in full uncut form. I played them both from beginning to end. They didn't sync. It was clear that Ted was lying in one or the other.

Marie and I looked at each other in dismay. How could someone whom we trusted implicitly pull a stunt like that—and then lie about it?

My mind began to race. "If Ted has this problem," I said to my wife, "do you think it has infected the rest of the staff? Is this really the DNA of New Life Church after all? If so, we've made a huge mistake. We've been fools."

There was no use trying to hide this from our daughters. I called them over to the computer and said, "There's really bad news about Pastor Ted. Watch these two interviews." I then played them both. "Look at what he's saying," I added. "He has to be lying."

"Yeah, he is!" they exploded. "We thought he was so great!" They were instantly furious.

"So there goes our youth group and all our new friends, Daddy!" one of them soon added. "We just got settled in there. I really like those kids, but what are we going to do now?"

"I honestly don't know, sweetheart," I replied. "This is absolutely a disaster."

By the weekend, the church's external board of overseers had swung into action, removing Ted Haggard from his position as senior pastor and calling for a full investigation. We looked at the board names and recognized Mike Ware, longtime pastor of Victory Church in northwest Denver, whom we had known and respected for years. Even the kids remembered him from the TV-studio evenings back in the mid-1990s. It gave us a great amount of comfort to know he was involved in sorting out this mess.

When we showed up for church on Sunday, November 5, we pushed our way past network media reporters and uplink trucks that choked the parking lots. That morning we would be part of the shell-shocked congregation hoping for a word of comfort and sanity. We listened that day to the letter of confession and apology that Pastor Ted had prepared for reading. We heard the overseers explain what they had discovered, and what would happen next. When the service ended, we cried and hugged our fellow worshipers like everyone else. Our hearts were broken, but at the same time we were starting to feel a little relief. Apparently the church was not going to collapse after all.

In time we became convinced that moral infection was *not* running wild through the staff. We felt we could continue to believe in Ross

Parsley, the music pastor who would now become interim senior pastor, and the others by his side. At one point I called a trusted pastor back in Montana for counsel, asking what he thought we should do. "I would encourage you to stay put," he answered. "You're a stable family. You can be of assistance to others in the congregation who are wavering these days."

On Tuesday, November 7, Colorado voters went to the polls and passed Amendment 43 (upholding traditional marriage) by a 55 to 45 percent margin. Referendum I (allowing domestic partnerships) went down to defeat, 48 to 52 percent. New Life Church meanwhile focused inward on moving forward and repairing the damage caused by Ted Haggard's actions.

If all this had happened a month or two earlier, when our family was still making up its mind about the church, we might have headed for the exits. But we had just cast our lot with this church family. We didn't feel we ought to reverse that decision. We would stay and help pick up the pieces.

Here We Go?

Our daughter Laurie was not home for this fiasco, having gone to a three-month Discipleship Training School (DTS) sponsored by Youth with a Mission (YWAM). Here she was plunged into classes on Christian doctrine, cross-cultural communication, and evangelistic methodology. She came home for Thanksgiving, then immediately headed off to the second half of her program, a fieldwork assignment teaching English in a closed country overseas. We would not see her again until March.

Stephanie was glad for her twin's venture, but at the same time, she felt a bit lost without Laurie around. She began reading all the more about world issues, especially the scourge of human trafficking. She grew to care deeply about social justice.

The two girls e-mailed each other constantly. No longer were they fussing over who liked which kinds of music; they were grappling with the hurts of a big violent planet. Laurie would describe what she was facing in her location; Stephanie would describe the latest book she had read on the Rwandan genocide. Their passion to heal the wounds of a broken world intensified.

At the same time, Marie and I were growing impatient for some kind of breakthrough in our own calling. We had been waiting an awfully long time for the chance to do what we believed God had planned for us. Standing in church one Sunday morning in our usual spot on the fourth row, I was struck by the reflective song the band was leading. It was titled "Who You Are," written by New Life's Jon Egan:

I won't be satisfied
I won't be found all right 'til I find
Who You are

I'd climb every mountain
I'd travel the deepest valley to find
Who You are

You, You cause the lame to walk
You open lips to talk
You're everything and that is who You are
You, You calm the storms at night
You turn the dark to light
You're everything and that is who You are.[3]

The longer the song went on, the more I began to complain in my thoughts. *God, we keep singing about all this stuff, all the incredible things You can do—but where is it? I don't want to just say the words. I want the reality.*

And in that moment, a strong impression burst upon my consciousness: *IT'S TIME TO SEE IT.* Yes! I couldn't agree more. I took this as a sign that awesome things were in store for New Life Church. I even shared this after the meeting with Pastor Ross. He welcomed the encouragement.

Over the next days and weeks, I came to feel that the impression applied in a personal sense, too, to us as a family. The long wait was just about over. I believed that God's greater work for us was just around the corner.

Nothing dramatic broke loose through the springtime, however. Our 20th anniversary came on May 2. We went to a bed-and-breakfast in Breckenridge to celebrate, finishing with a special dinner at our favorite restaurant in Vail, the Swiss Chalet at the Sonnenalp Resort. A warm fire crackled in the fireplace. A big cuckoo clock kept time in the background. We looked at each other across the table, and once again we were drawn to this phrase: *It's time to see it.* We talked at length about how God wanted to do great things with us. The vision from long ago would surely come to pass soon. We felt we were on the verge of something wondrous in our lives.

WORLD TRAVELERS

By now, Laurie was back from her YWAM experience. She suddenly seemed all grown up to us. She was much more interested in making her own decisions. This was normal, we told each other, for an 18-year-old who had been 11 time zones away by herself.

She got a job as a barista at Peaberry's, a nearby coffee spot. Sometime around Memorial Day, the whole family went to a different Peaberry's for a talk about how things were going. The conversation centered on our communication patterns. Rachel in particular was fairly forthright.

"Dad, I sometimes feel you're not really paying attention to us individually. I feel like I'm not heard. For example, I have this dream about going to New Zealand someday and opening up a place for teenage girls who are depressed. Did you know that New Zealand has the highest percentage of teen female suicides in the world? I really want to do something about this; I'm not just kidding around. And I don't think you're tracking with me. You're not taking me seriously."

Stephanie talked about wanting to move to France and live there long enough to learn the language. She was also eyeing a finishing school next door in Switzerland, one of the few left in the world, where she could learn everything from protocol to international relations.

Laurie opened up about some of her dreams as well.

I got the clear picture that they wished their dad would listen more and talk less. I've always been the most verbal one in our family. Now the girls had their own speeches to make. They were not resisting the long-held vision of our family doing something overseas together. They fully supported that, but in the meantime they had individual dreams they wanted to pursue and needs to be met in order to pursue them.

We talked for two hours in the coffee shop that morning, and even more in the car afterward. Stephanie and Laurie said they really wanted my help as they prepared for the upcoming SATs, so they could look their best on college applications. I promised to make time for this. I apologized for the ways I had neglected them in recent years, particularly during the time of Gramps's passing and then during the complicated ordeal of settling his estate, which took more than a year. I told them I hadn't wanted to ignore them, but rather I wanted to release them toward whatever God had in mind for their futures.

The tone of the conversation never got ugly, but the dialogue was brisk. This was, in one sense, a different angle on "It's time to *see it*." I needed to see what was lacking in my service as a father. In the weeks that followed the Peaberry morning, we made definite, if gradual, progress. We got more in tune with each other's hearts and ambitions.

In June Rachel left for another mission trip with Teen Mania, this time to Mexico. Then on the first Friday night of July, I was with the girls at theMILL back at New Life Church when Pastor Aaron Stern stood up with an unusual announcement: "Guess what, everybody. We've just had a situation develop over the last 48 hours that I need to tell you about. There's a summer camp for Chinese young people that starts in just a few weeks in Beijing, and the government's plan has been to have a mix of Western counterparts there too. They apparently want an exchange of ideas and understanding. They want the camp to center on leadership skills, moral concepts, and so on.

"But several churches that were supposed to be lining up the American kids haven't been able to come up with enough students. Now here at the last minute, we've been asked if we can fill the gap. I know it's ridiculously late to be bringing this up, but if you're interested in finding out more, come to a meeting afterward in room [such-and-such]."

I sat there stunned. *Beijing—the first city with the glowing red light in my vision 22 years ago!* Could this be? Surely not.

Within seconds I became aware of three sets of young eyes staring in my direction: Stephanie's, Laurie's, and Rachel's. They mouthed the words across the auditorium: *Can we go?!* I gave them a hopeful shrug that indicated we should at least attend the information session to follow.

We found out the group would need to leave Colorado in two weeks, which allowed almost no time for fund-raising. Aaron said, "All we can do is stand up in church this Sunday, explain the opportunity, and then take an offering. Whatever amount of money comes in will determine how many students we can send." In the meantime, there was an application form to fill out. My girls quickly grabbed copies and began scribbling.

The car was full of excited conversation on the drive home that night. "We already have our passports, Dad!" they reminded me. They buzzed all the way to Denver about how cool this was going to be. I offered the viewpoint that if only one from our family was chosen to go, it should be Stephanie. She hadn't yet been on a mission trip, whereas the other two had. Laurie and Rachel agreed to that.

When the Sunday offering was collected and counted, the result was astounding. New Life could afford to send 76 kids. Within a day or two, the names of approved applicants were posted. All three of our girls made the cut.

It was a mad scramble getting ready to board the plane. But the trip turned out to be incredible. During 10 days at the camp, our girls mingled with Chinese young people their age and had fascinating conversations. Stephanie especially reached out to a number of girls. One was the daughter of a provincial governor. They exchanged e-mail addresses and promised to keep in touch with each other.

Rachel, for the first time in her life, got to do archery—a dream of hers ever since reading The Lord of the Rings series. (LOTR was an obsession for Rachel. She and Aimee, her friend from Virginia whom she met on the 2005 Teen Mania trip to Brazil, even learned Elvish!) Then one evening when she was feeling particularly homesick, she went outside to a playground. While praying, she heard a little boy crying on a swing set. She felt led to go hug him. She initially shrugged off the feeling, but eventually she followed through.

The little Chinese boy, who could speak English, told how he was missing his family. She told him that she missed her family too, but that God is always with us. The boy stopped crying when he heard this, and a warm smile lit up his face. Despite the difficulty of being in a new and strange culture, Rachel was able to help one small boy.

When the camp wrapped up, the girls' group took an overnight train south to Hong Kong, where they spent a day or two seeing the sights, shopping, and going to the beach. They arrived back home in early August, jet-lagged but still exuberant about all they had done. Laurie and Rachel reported that they had never seen Stephanie so happy. "She was totally in her element," one said. "She absolutely thrived in this environment. The two of us were a little more tentative, but she was completely fearless."

Marie and I couldn't stop smiling for days. God was using our girls in ways and in specific places we had long dreamed about. Another part of "it," we joyfully told ourselves.

LIFE—AND DEATH

Three trips out of the country had definitely made Rachel think about the major questions of life. In her journal, she revealed what was on her mind on August 15, 2007:

> I think I have become impulsive, but in a good way. Not in buying things, but doing things I've always wanted to do. I probably never wrote this down anywhere, but I've always wanted to walk down to Fairmount Cemetery [Denver's largest, not far from our apartment]. Yesterday and this morning I finally figured out a way. I walked there this afternoon, and it was one of the greatest things I've ever done.
>
> I haven't been in a cemetery since Coco [a member of our church] died back in Montana. It's a sobering experience really. Seeing people who have lived their lives and died, it brings death to, yet again, a reality. Death has been thrown at me in numerous ways. Gramps died back in 2004. David this summer,[4] and now my ramble in a

graveyard. There were big monuments, smaller ones, and ones you barely noticed. I felt sorry for the little ones.

I also saw a fresh grave. Fresh flowers rested on it, red roses, carnations, and another flower I don't know the name of. I think I'll keep going back to that one until it gets a gravestone and I know who it is.

My ultimate goal is to someday find [Columbine victim] Isaiah Shoels's grave, although since there are so many graves and he's only one person, I wonder if I will find him. I've always felt such an odd connection to him. He was the only student that died at Columbine that I cried for. You'd think I'd have cried more over Rachel Scott . . . being connected by name, but I only remember crying over Isaiah Shoels. I wonder what connected me so much to him. I would like to find out.

Yes, it has been a good day.

The next day, Rachel added this observation:

August 16, 2007

Aimee asked me why I've always wanted to go to that cemetery. She said it was kind of creepy. I think a person has to have a good view of both sides, life and death. Do not fear death, but also do not fear life. Fearing death might keep you from living, but fearing life will keep you from living. Live as though the end is death, but do not be afraid. Death is simply the beginning of another path. Another world, where Jesus is King.

We never saw these notations, of course, until much later.

PEACE AND GOOD WILL

That same month of August, the New Life pastoral search committee wrapped up their research and introduced their recommendation for the next senior pastor. Excitement swelled as we got to meet the Reverend Brady Boyd, an articulate 40-year-old minister from the Dallas-Fort Worth area. His gracious manner and humble attitude impressed us right away as he spoke for three consecutive Sundays, after which the congregation voted. It was overwhelmingly positive. We looked forward to the healing touch he would bring to this wounded but hopeful congregation.

He had a background in sports broadcasting before he had entered the ministry, and you could tell it by how easily the words flowed. He could obviously think on his feet and handle just about any question thrown at him. Yet he wasn't plastic; he conveyed a trustworthiness that made you know he was speaking honestly from the heart. Our girls liked him right away, and so did we.

Throughout the fall, life rolled along smoothly in the Works household. For Grace's 11th birthday right after Thanksgiving, we took four friends plus our family to an ice skating rink. It was a great time of fun. "We have to do this again!" said Rachel and Stephanie.

Rachel had lined up a trip to Virginia starting December 10 to visit Aimee. Being home-schooled, she could afford to bend the schedule in this way.

Christmastime landed upon us before we were ready. We didn't manage to get our decorations up as early as normal, although we pulled them out of storage and had the boxes near at hand. During the first full week of December, Laurie got called to work extra shifts at Peaberry's to cover for two employees with various family emergencies. She was too exhausted, in fact, to go to theMILL on Friday night, December 7—a rare miss for her.

Marie, Stephanie, and Rachel went on to Colorado Springs without her. Along the highway, they adjusted their plans, dropping Rachel at the church while Marie and Stephanie headed to a nearby mall for some shopping. They came home late saying it had been a frustrating time; the stores closed earlier than they had expected during the Christmas season, and Stephanie couldn't find the shoes she had hoped to buy.

I had spent the evening at home catching up on chores, while Grace read and watched TV with Laurie. Along the way, I stopped by my computer two or three times to scan various news sites. I was curious to get more details on the Wednesday mall shooting that had happened in Omaha, where a 19-year-old gunman had walked into the Westroads Mall and opened fire, killing eight before taking his own life. I knew the place well; it was right across the boulevard from the Marriott where I stayed whenever I went on business to our First Data offices there.

The mother of one of this kid's few friends now said he "reminded me of a lost puppy that nobody wanted." He had recently broken up with his girlfriend. *What a senseless tragedy*, I thought to myself. I wondered if any of our First Data people had ties to the victims, who just happened to be in the wrong place at the wrong time.

Saturday passed uneventfully for our family, as Rachel busied herself getting ready for her trip the next week. We went to sleep that night looking forward to the peace and blessing that another Sunday at New Life Church would no doubt bring.

ONE SNOWY SUNDAY

As soon as we got up the next morning and looked out the window, we saw the falling snow. It wasn't a blizzard by any means, but it would be enough to slow down the traffic on the way to church. "Okay, everybody," I (David) announced to the household, "we need to get on the road earlier this morning—like 9:30. Keep an eye on the clock." Making sure four girls got up, dressed, fed, and out the door on time was a challenge any week, even without the weather factor. At least one of the crew always seemed to be perplexed about what to wear.

While waiting for bathroom access, I stopped by my computer to check the overnight news. According to 9NEWS.com, there had been an incident around midnight at the Youth with a Mission center in Arvada, a northwest suburb of Denver. We knew a lot about YWAM in general, but we had never been to this particular facility, some 25 miles across the city. I knew it was in a residential area close to Faith Bible Chapel.

The news blurb was short; it sounded like a robbery attempt. Two had been killed, and several others injured. The assailant was apparently still at large.

What in the world?! I thought to myself. *They haven't caught the guy yet? He's still running around the neighborhood? That's strange.*

"Marie, look at this," I said. "Some guy tried to barge into YWAM over in Arvada and ended up killing two people."

"You're kidding!"

"No, that's what it says here," I said as I glanced at the time stamp on the screen. "Channel 9 posted this story back at three o'clock in the morning—but they haven't updated it since then. They don't say what's the deal on finding the shooter."

There wasn't time to continue surfing the Internet for more information. We had to get on our way if we were going to make the 11 o'clock service in Colorado Springs. We loaded ourselves into the minivan, our pearl white 2005 Toyota Sienna known in the family as "Mom's car," since she had been the one to pick it out in the beginning. Marie drove, while I sat in the front passenger seat. In the middle of the van were two captain's chairs that folded down, with a console between them. Directly behind Marie sat Stephanie; directly behind me sat Rachel. In the far back was Grace on the left side, Laurie on the right.

Interstate 25 was slushy enough to command Marie's full attention. The rest of us were quieter than usual that morning, probably because of the weather. By the time we passed over Monument Hill (the high point between Denver and "the Springs," as it's called), the window washer fluid was gone because of the constant splashing from other cars. "I can't see what I'm doing—I'm going to stop for some more fluid," Marie said.

"Really?" I replied. "Can't we make it the rest of the way and do that after church? I don't want to be late."

"No, I really need a clear windshield," she said. She pulled off at the exit for Monument, a small town eight miles north of the church, to refill the washer fluid at a gas station. Soon we were back on the highway.

The snow kept falling. When we entered the church complex, the parking lots were busy as the first-service crowd of several thousand was exiting and we second-service people were hovering to get our spaces. Marie drove around to the back side of the building in hopes of finding a closer spot. She was successful; we pulled into a space less than 40 feet from a door. It would be a long walk down the wide hallway before we reached the worship center, but at least we'd be indoors.

On the way in, I said to my wife, "Maybe we'll find somebody here who knows more about what happened at YWAM." The organization maintained a small office in the World Prayer Center building on the church campus.

Once we got situated in the sanctuary, Marie turned to Laurie, our daughter with the most YWAM experience, and said, "Dad saw something on the news this morning about a shooting up at the YWAM base in Arvada. Do you know any kids who are there now?"

Laurie's eyes grew wide. "Yes!" she cried. "My friend Tina is there. She was in my DTS class last fall. She's from England." Laurie dashed out of our row to return to the outer concourse, where she could begin calling or texting friends to find out what was going on. The rest of us stayed in place for the service that was about to start.

A HEART FOR CHRISTMAS

The worship center was ablaze with Christmas color as well as props and backdrops for *Wonderland*, the musical that had already run for several performances throughout the weekend and would be back on stage the following weekend as well. The praise-and-worship time that morning was refreshing for us all. A guest speaker had come that day, the well-known Jack Hayford from Church on the Way in Van Nuys, California, whom we had seen dozens of times on television. A tall, balding man in his seventies, he had written more than 50 books and a number of musical compositions, including the classic worship chorus "Majesty."

He read his biblical text from the Gospel of Matthew, chapter 2—the story of the Wise Men coming to see the Christ Child—and began talking about the importance of what he called "a soft heart." I pulled out my pad and began taking notes. He pointed out the four actions of verse 11: "They *bowed down* and *worshiped* him. Then they *opened their treasures* and *presented him with gifts* of gold and of incense and of myrrh" (emphasis added).

All this, Hayford said, was in contrast to the Jerusalem authorities and scholars in previous verses, who discussed and debated the facts but had no heart for what was going on in Bethlehem. They didn't recognize that the Messiah had come. The Wise Men, on the other hand, were overwhelmed to the point of falling prostrate. They freely gave their worship and adoration as well as their gifts.

"Softheartedness is not the same as softheadedness," the speaker pointed out. "A soft heart is shapeable. It is eminently correctable. It can be imprinted. It is patient. It is forgiving." He told several stories and then concluded his message with an invitation for each of us to pray, "Lord, on this Christmas give me a softer heart than ever before."

When the service ended sometime after 12:30, we hung around the sanctuary and reconnected with Laurie. By now she had learned that her friend Tina was safe, although shaken by what had occurred. Beyond that, information was scarce. I asked several people if they had additional details on the Arvada incident. I checked with Pastor Evan Martin, one of the leaders of theMILL who had been instrumental in our girls going to China. Nobody seemed to have any fresh news.

The church was starting to clear out. We gradually gathered our clan, walked out of the sanctuary, and began ambling down the long corridor. As usual, we were among the stragglers taking their time getting out the door after the morning service.

"Where shall we go for lunch?" I asked. "How about Good Times?" (a nearby hamburger restaurant).

"Aw, Dad, we went there just a couple of weeks ago," Laurie said. "How about someplace different?"

"Like where?"

"I don't know." We tried to think of an alternative that everyone would like, but didn't get very far. In the end, I said, "Well, looks to me like Good Times is still in first place. Let's go." With that, we pulled our coats tighter around us and headed out into the winter chill, shuffling carefully across the snowy spots. The flakes had stopped falling by now, and the sun had appeared. But the cold breeze still stung our faces, since few vehicles remained in the parking lot to block the wind.

Jessie Gingrich, a family friend just a few years older than our teenagers, was at her car, which was nose-to-nose with ours, only one spot to the left. "Hey look, there's Jessie," Rachel said. Laurie, Stephanie, and Rachel all waved and said, "Hi."

As we neared the van, Laurie appeared to be headed for the left-side sliding door.

"No, no—you have to sit in the back on the other side," Rachel corrected. Our family didn't have assigned seats, but the tradition was that you kept the same seat for both parts of a trip, going and coming. If you started out the day in a certain seat, you had to stick to it. Laurie had ridden down to church in the right rear seat of the van, and Rachel was determined to keep her in line.

"Okay, okay," Laurie responded as she walked around the back of the van and entered through the right-side sliding door. Meanwhile, the rest of us got situated: Grace beside Laurie in the back, Stephanie in the left-side middle, Marie in the driver's seat, and I beside her in the front passenger seat. Rachel paused for a moment at the right-side entrance to the van, digging for some item in her purse.

UNDER FIRE

Crack! Something metallic made a sharp sound. *What was that?*

I let go of the seat belt I had been trying to buckle and turned to look toward where the sound had come from. I was confused. Was it from behind us? I swiveled my head toward the right side again, surveying the parking lot.

And there he was—a skinny young guy maybe 20 yards away, dressed in black, even to the knit hat he wore on his head. He was toting a fearsome-looking rifle, which he raised again to fire in our direction. *What in the world! This doesn't make any sense!* Another shot rang out and hit something, making a loud sound.

I didn't have time to realize what this meant. All I could do was scream to my family, "Get down! Get down! There's a shooter out there! He's shooting at us!" I crouched down into the footwell in front of my seat, trying to get as low as possible. The others did the same, screaming as they went. I tried to think of something spiritual to pray. At that moment, a bullet hit the window above my head. Glass flew. In terror I screamed out, "Dear God, save us!"

The shots kept ringing out; the noise was thunderous. We were in a shooting gallery with no room to maneuver. More shots went screaming past. The angle of the sound told me that the shooter was on the move now toward the front of our van and on toward the church building. He had started out maybe eight car spaces away; now he was only half that distance.

Just like Omaha, I thought to myself. *Another messed-up kid working out his "issues."* And then a new theory hit my brain: *Is this a copycat of what happened last night in Arvada? These news stories have a way of duplicating themselves.*

Wait a minute—where was Rachel? She hadn't yet climbed into the van when the shooting had started. I squirmed around to try to see her. There she was, still standing on the snowy parking lot with a dazed look on her face. In her burnt orange T-shirt with the strip of sunrise pattern across the bottom, there was a hole penetrating her lower-right rib cage.

"Rachel!" I cried out.

"I think I've been shot," she said weakly.

And then, she collapsed backwards in a heap on the blacktop.

Little Gracie let out a new scream and scrambled her way over Laurie's legs to get out of the backseat and help her fallen sister. I pulled my door handle to jump out and do the same. My feet hit the ground, but before I could kneel down at Rachel's side—*zip!*—a fresh volley of bullets went whizzing past my head. I whirled to look over my shoulder and was horrified to see the gunman no more than 10 yards in front of me, with his AR-15-style rifle pointed right at me.

I turned to dive out of the line of fire. A pain shot through my abdomen, right above my belt line on the right side. I wanted to move toward Rachel, but . . . ooh . . . my midsection really hurt. *Wait a minute—I've been shot too,* I realized. *God, this can't be happening!*

In the split second between realizing I had been shot and actually hitting the pavement, time slowed down. I knew I was hurt but assumed I would be okay. Rachel, on the other hand, was in bad shape.

God, what's going on here? This is crazy. We're supposed to be a missionary family getting ready to go around the world for You. What's this all about? It doesn't make any sense.

And in that moment, I felt a sense of understanding from God. It wasn't an audible voice by any means. The words simply came into my mind: *We're going THROUGH. We're not going OVER or going AROUND this. We're going THROUGH.*

That obviously was not what I wanted to hear. I lay on my stomach to lessen the pain and to attempt to stop the bleeding that was obviously going on. It was the only way I knew to keep direct pressure on the wounds. It also was the most comfortable position.

"Gracie, get down and play dead!" I ordered my youngest daughter. "He's still here!" The shots kept ringing out. With every pause, I hoped it would be the last. But then another volley . . .

The shots stopped momentarily. Then they resumed, but more distant now, more muffled. We all held our breath.

He's gone inside the church, I thought. *There's still lots of people in there. Oh no—it's going to be a bloodbath. Oh, God, stop him!*

I stretched out my arm in Rachel's direction, trying to will my body to move, even crawl. It simply hurt too much. She needed her father, her protector . . . and I couldn't get to her side. "I'm so sorry, honey— I can't reach you," I said through tears.

"That's okay, Daddy," she whispered.

I kept lying on my stomach looking sideways toward Rachel. The moment was almost surreal, like in an old Western movie where all dialogue stops and you can only hear the wind blowing a few tumbleweeds across the prairie. *God, don't let us die out here on a cold parking lot*, I prayed.

MOTHER AND CHILD

As soon as the shots died down, I (Marie) squeezed myself through the gap in the front seats and out onto the blacktop where Rachel lay. Her eyes were open with a look of pain. I had no idea how to help her. As a mom, I knew how to handle skinned knees and bee stings—but nothing of this magnitude. It was in this moment that I shut down my emotions. I knew by faith that my heavenly Father would come to help if I asked Him. So I cried out to God, "Send Your angels to help us!" After all, we needed both natural and supernatural help. In the next moments, I had the very real sense of my heavenly Father swooping in and beginning to carry us.

Rachel seemed calm as she lay there. She hadn't actually put her coat on, and I worried about her being cold. Should I try to cover her up? But what if I caused more injury? Meanwhile, Gracie kept crying and hovering over her.

Other people were rushing to help us in this moment, and so my attention diverted to Stephanie. During the hail of bullets I had heard her trying to crouch down in her seat. When I came to the open door, I was surprised to see her lying facedown, draped across the middle console in an awkward position. Her feet were in fact on her original seat on the left side, while her shoulders and head were almost touching the floor on the right side. How had she landed in such a contortion?

Laurie, in the right rear seat and unharmed, was by now on the phone to 9-1-1. "There's a shooting at New Life—New Life Church! There's someone shooting at us!"

"Where are you, inside or outside?"

"Outside."

"Has anyone been injured?"

(Gasping) "Yes! My sister—my twin sister, and my younger sister!"

"Okay, hold on. I'm going to send police, fire, and medical."

I reached out to Stephanie and saw a bullet hole in the back of her left shoulder. Oddly enough, it was not bleeding. That puzzled me. I gently turned her head and shoulders. She was limp; her eyes were closed, as if she was asleep. To my horror, I saw a large clot of blood coming out of her nose. The side of her face was bloody as well, all the way to her ear. I took a deep breath and thought, *Oh no! She's been shot in the head!* But, I could see no actual bullet impact. I tried to clear my mind and figure out what to do next.

I reached down for her wrist, checking for a pulse. I could feel nothing in my fingertips. I then tried to find a pulse in her neck. I didn't want to believe she was gone, but I couldn't find any evidence that her heart was still pumping.

On the phone, the operator wanted to know if Laurie had seen who shot us. "No!" she replied, now crying convulsively. Grace's screams continued in the background.

"Can you possibly move away from where the shooter is?"

"No! We've got three people down from my family. We can't move!"

"All right. Is there any serious bleeding? If so, I need for you to put a cloth on, put pressure to control the bleeding."

Laurie turned to instruct me. "Mom, you have to control the bleeding!"

"I don't know *where*!" I answered. "I don't think it's going to help. I can't find a pulse."

Laurie found her scarf and shoved it at me, insisting, "Here, take my scarf. Put pressure on the wound!"

I could see no bleeding gunshot wound to treat, even on Stephanie's face. I didn't know how to follow through on the operator's direction. I grabbed hold of Stephanie's upper torso and struggled to turn her over so I could investigate further. It was very difficult.

The more I saw of her closed eyes, the more it began to hit me that she was actually unconscious. I kept looking in vain for a place to apply pressure with the scarf. Suddenly, a young man's hand reached over me to take my hand with the scarf and apply it to her upper-right rib cage. I still don't know who the young man was; he must have sensed my confusion and stepped in to help. Then he disappeared as quickly as he had come.

"Is your sister still breathing?" the operator wanted to know. Neither Laurie nor I could say for sure.

"Is she choking on her blood?"

"No," Laurie reported through her sobs. "She's not conscious."

"Okay, we do have help on the way," the operator assured her. She asked for a description of our van, then told us to turn on our hazard lights for quick identification as soon as emergency personnel arrived.

Laurie jumped out of the van at this point to head for the front seat and do this, while I kept holding Stephanie's limp body.

Call it mother's intuition or whatever you want: I somehow knew even at this early moment that Stephanie was not going to make it. I had no medical proof. I didn't yet know what I would later learn, that the hole in her left shoulder was actually an exit wound. A bullet had entered her right torso and ripped a deadly path through her lungs and heart chamber as it crossed her body. I didn't know that the facial blood was in fact superficial; she had slammed her head down onto the console so hard she had given herself a nosebleed, and then I had spread the blood across her cheek in the process of turning her. Even so, I could sense something final in this instant. My firstborn was dying.

By now, police officers were swarming around, followed quickly by ambulance personnel. I grabbed the arm of a tall EMT named Doug McIntyre and said, "Please—help her! She's the worst."

He glanced at Stephanie and replied, "Yes, okay." Almost apologetically he continued, "I'm really sorry, but we're going to need some room to work on her. Could you maybe step out?"

I got out of the van. Standing in the parking lot, I could only see his back and those of his partners. Not until days later did I learn what actually went on in the next few minutes. His first move had been to hook up a heart monitor. He quickly applied adhesive patches to both her arms and both legs. He attached the wires and then studied the monitor carefully.

He began checking her wounds and came across the entrance wound, which by now was bleeding profusely. He watched the monitor's ever-weakening signal. The heart was gradually shutting down. Doug gave a serious glance at his teammate. He looked back at the monitor once again and let out a small sigh. His shoulders slumped as he disconnected the wires.

He then did something entirely outside medical protocol. He bowed his head and recited the Lord's Prayer. Then he raised his right hand to make the sign of the cross. He had no way of knowing that Stephanie was a traditionalist who would have loved that. He was simply committing her to the care of the Great Shepherd from this point onward.

I stood watching, waiting for a confirmation of what I believed in my heart but couldn't verify on my own. I was determined to know for sure. My hands hung heavy at my sides. I was transfixed, even numb. I couldn't cry out or go into panic mode; I was once again the little girl staring blankly at my stricken mother the day the water heater blew up. Only this time I knew my heavenly Father was here and was carrying us. He had heard my call for help. Stephanie would be all right with Him in their heavenly home.

A doctor who had been present in the church service, Brian Olivier, had come on the scene by now. Seeing the EMTs pull back, he did the only thing left to preserve Stephanie's dignity and privacy. He brought out a white hand towel—from where I don't know—and gently covered her face.

HANGING BY
A THREAD

By now more people were running toward us from the church as well as their cars, wanting to help. They were praying aloud as they swarmed around us and held us close. Doug McIntyre and his team of EMTs quickly turned their attention to Rachel, while a second team focused on David.

"Hey, I've got a pulse again!" the EMT working on Rachel called out. Her color, however, was gray, and she looked awful lying there on the ground. Within seconds, a backboard was brought to carry her. Once they lifted her inside the shelter of the ambulance, Doug turned to ask when the Flight for Life helicopter would arrive. He assumed he would have this support at any moment and was irritated to find that none was coming. They would have to make the 12-mile trip south to Penrose Hospital by road instead.

The ambulance went racing out of the parking lot in a double hurry—not only was Rachel in critical condition, but for all anyone knew, the shooter could reappear at any time. Inside the vehicle (we heard the story later), the three-man crew was alarmed to find that her pulse had faded out again. Doug quickly inserted an IV in her arm while one partner began pumping oxygen into her airway using a bag-mask resuscitator. The third EMT located the entrance wound on the left side of her chest and was relieved to see little blood loss occurring.

A minute or so passed, the ambulance still roaring down the interstate. Suddenly, Rachel's color began to return, rising from her midsection up to her face. "It was like the sun coming out after a spring rain," Doug told us. "She became . . . beautiful again. We were mesmerized.

"Then . . . she opened her eyes. She began tracking our movements. We didn't stop doing the CPR or pushing the fluids, but we were just astounded. She was literally glowing; there was an aura around her, it seemed. We had her back again!

"I spoke to her. 'We're the emergency medical team, and we're taking you to the hospital. You're safe now. You're going to be okay.' She seemed to understand. I thought I saw some of the fear start to fade from her eyes."

The crew members stared at this resurrection right before them, and a sense of peace filled the ambulance. A minute or two passed . . . but then Rachel began to fade again. The crew pushed their interventions all the harder. "We've got to bring her back!" they told one another.

Again, she revived. "You're going to be okay," Doug whispered in her ear. "God is with you. God will give you the strength." He felt like he was caring for his own child or sister. It wasn't politically correct for an EMT to get this attached to his patient or to show this kind of feeling, but he didn't care. He and his team were determined not to lose her.

At one point Rachel even attempted to speak. Her words were hard to understand, but they did catch the word "God."

What else could be done? They decided on an intubation. Doug leaned down to explain. "I have to put a tube in your throat to breathe for you, because I'm worried that the bullet might have hit one of your lungs. I'll give you some medicine first so you don't gag. This is to help you." Rachel blinked her eyes to show that she understood.

The procedure went smoothly, and by the time the ambulance screeched into Penrose's emergency dock, she was looking strong. Her heart rate was stable, her blood pressure was in a good range, her color was in bloom, she was moving her eyes. The hospital attendants whisked her straight toward surgery, but not before Doug said one last time to her, "You're doing great. God's helping you. Stay strong."

The three tough EMTs then walked back outside into the parking lot and "cried like babies," Doug admitted later. "We each called our loved ones and told them how much we loved them. We were exhausted, but at the same time, we were sure we had saved this girl's life."

DAD'S TURN

While all this was taking place, another medical crew was attending to me (David) on the ground. "What happened?" an EMT asked me. "Where does it hurt?"

"I got shot in the belly," I answered.

"Okay, we need to turn you over and check it out."

I didn't want to turn over because I knew from my Boy Scout days that pressure on a wound was a good thing, and if I relieved the pressure on my abdomen, it would hurt worse. I didn't have a choice, however. In fact, Dr. Olivier was already running a pair of scissors up the back of my blue winter coat, my oxford button-down shirt, and my T-shirt underneath as well. Next came the cutting of my brand-new, never-worn-before L.L.Bean khaki pants and my underwear. They rolled me over—and there I was, naked in front of God and everybody in the parking lot. Couldn't they have waited to do this inside an ambulance? Only my shoes and socks remained in place.

It was cold. It was embarrassing. They began probing the bullet holes. It hurt like crazy. I tried to hold back the pain, until one of them gave me permission to let go. I started yelling.

I didn't yet realize at that point that whereas Stephanie and Rachel had taken only one bullet each, I had taken two. The shot to the groin didn't hurt as much as the shot across the stomach.

I looked around and saw an entire ring of cops with their guns drawn, all on one knee facing outward like a perimeter guard encircling the wagons in the Old West. If there was a second or third shooter— no one knew for sure yet—they wanted to be ready. I saw other faces above me in a blur. I recognized Joe Kirkendall, the teaching pastor of theMILL. "Here, take my cell phone," I said. "I don't want it to get lost out here. Call people and ask them to pray!"

Fortunately, before this Laurie and Grace had been removed from the scene. Someone had talked them into getting out of the cold by jumping into a nearby pickup truck. This was also wise in case the shooting wasn't yet over. Gracie had gone screaming at the top of her lungs, completely terrorized, while Laurie began hyperventilating. It broke my heart to see them so hysterical. I said to myself, *Everything is now out of my control, isn't it? I can't change anything. I have to go along with whatever other people decide.*

While the EMTs worked, a police officer knelt down to talk to me. "Did you get to see the shooter?"

"Yes—just for a second or two."

"Did you recognize him?"

"No. I have no idea—"

"Is there anybody you know who would have come after you?"

"No. I can't think of anyone in my life who would do something like this."

Mercifully, I was soon loaded onto a backboard and carried into an ambulance. On the trip down the interstate, I felt every bump in the road. I heard the conversation up front about which of Colorado Springs' hospitals to go to. They settled on Penrose hospital where Rachel had been taken.

An EMT kept trying to put an IV in my arm. It wouldn't work. Finally they resorted to inserting it into my neck. The pain medication was definitely welcome.

Otherwise, I found a bit of respite by closing my eyes. The sensory input had been cascading ever since the first gunshot. I needed to shut out some of the flashing lights, the people rushing around, the medical tubing, and all the rest. If I didn't look at these things, I could regain some of my composure.

Once inside the emergency room, however, I had to resume paying attention. They quickly checked me over and gave me more and stronger pain medication through the IV. A police detective tried to ask me some questions, but I was fairly incoherent. Dr. Scott Fisher, a tall, brown-haired, younger-than-I surgeon in blue scrubs, soon came alongside and began examining my midsection. "Okay, this appears to be the entrance wound," he said, pointing to the hole in my lower right side. "And this is the exit wound," he added as he touched the hole just to the left of my navel. "Then down here in your upper leg and groin area—wow, you are really lucky. It did some damage, but it missed the femoral artery. "The good news is that none of these are life threatening, although I don't want to minimize the pain you are feeling. "We're going to need to take you into surgery and make sure we get all the foreign material out. Bullets are not sterile, you know." He even cracked a little joke by saying, "The bad guys don't usually take time to sterilize their bullets." We both smiled at that.

"Before we do the surgery, though, we want to do an MRI."

Following that procedure, there was time for me to be interviewed by another Colorado Springs Police Department detective, Donald Chagnon. He was a very calm man, who despite being all business, was also visibly moved by what had occurred. He began taking notes as I told everything I could recall about this awful day.

I told him I wouldn't recognize the shooter if I were to see him again. I then asked, "Does this have anything to do with what happened up in Arvada last night?"

"We're not sure at this point," he answered. "But we wouldn't be surprised. We're definitely pursuing that line of inquiry."

We kept getting interrupted by nurses and other medical people attending to me. And my pain level was still high enough that I was foggy on more than a few details. In fact, I lost consciousness a couple of times, interrupting the interview. I heard the word *morphine* a time or two—a good word, under the circumstances.

So Few?

One thought was clear in my mind, however. This ER should have been much busier by now. Staff members seemed to be just waiting around. Why weren't there dozens more victims being brought through the doors?

Across the way, the staff was working on one woman from the church who had taken a bullet in the shoulder; we later learned her name was Judy Purcell. She had been shot at close range inside her vehicle as she and her family drove past ours. Her husband had jammed down the gas pedal and had driven her straight to the hospital. It turned out she wasn't seriously injured.

Other than Judy, where were the rest? I was fairly sure the shooter had gotten inside the church, where people would have had little chance to avoid him. I assumed it must have been horrific in there. I finally asked a nurse, "How come we're not getting lots more people in here with gunshot wounds? The guy was firing all over the place."

"Well," she discreetly replied, "whoever it was is dead now."

"What do you mean? All that gunfire—surely more people got hit than just us."

"No, this is everyone," she replied.

I was confused. It would be the next day, of course, before I would learn the dramatic details of how New Life Church security guard Jeanne Assam bravely brought down the shooter in the corridor before he could devastate any more people.

A phone was brought to me. My sister, Linnaea, was calling from Utah. "David, I'm so, so sorry. We're heading for the airport; I'll be on the very next plane."

"Oh, you don't need to come out," I replied in my uninformed state. "We'll be all right. I've just got a flesh wound, and I think Rachel is going to be okay."

"No, I'm coming," Linnaea said. She was firm.

By the time I was wheeled from the ER into the preparation room just before surgery, I was making less sense than ever. Pastor Brady was standing there, deep concern in his eyes. He reached out to touch my arm and said, "David, we have the whole church praying for you and your family. We have pastors here looking after Marie and the girls. We're here for you, brother."

I turned to him and blurted out the dumbest remark. I said, "Hey, I just want you to know I'm not going to sue the church!"

He looked at me oddly, paused a second, and then got the conversation back on track. "Okay . . . why don't we have a word of prayer before you go into surgery?" He then prayed for God to watch over me and give the doctors skill in operating. Soon afterward, I was on my way to oblivion for a while.

WAITING AND WONDERING

For the two girls and me (Marie), it had been perplexing to be detained at the church instead of heading straight to the hospital. Shortly after the first ambulance left, we had been moved into the nearby building known as "the Tent"—actually, it's a metal structure with a rounded roofline that has a large foyer and an auditorium that seats maybe 500 people. At least we would be safe there, we were told.

It took the authorities a while to figure out who we actually were: family members of the main victims. They eventually came to interview us briefly. Dr. Olivier and his wife, Shelley, stayed near us, as well as a woman named Renae Culver, who was especially kind to stick with Grace.

I turned to the doctor's wife with a question that was tormenting me.

"Do you think it was all right for me to have moved Stephanie like I did? Did I hurt anything?"

"You did the right thing," she assured me. "It was okay—really."

"Well, I couldn't find a pulse. I had to do something. But I'm pretty sure she didn't make it."

Laurie was nearby talking on the phone with her boyfriend, Jesse Klopfenstein, who had been snowboarding in the mountains. At my statement, she turned away and put her finger in her right ear; she couldn't bear to hear my conclusion. I didn't press the point with her.

Soon Pastor Brady arrived to see how everyone was doing. "I'm so sorry," he said. "Your church family is going to stand with you through this." He then gathered us all into a circle for prayer.

I was still stunned, but I summoned enough composure to call my mother in Nebraska.

"Mom, this is Marie. Did you hear about the shooting at our church in Colorado Springs?"

"Yes," she answered. "There was something about that on the radio, I think. . . ."

"Well—it was us that got shot! Stephanie is gone. David and Rachel were both shot too. I think David is okay, but I'm not sure about Rachel."

"Oh, Marie!" she cried.

She told me she would call David's mother in Kansas City right away to let her know. That would trigger calls to his sister in Utah and his brother in Denver. I promised to call my mother back when I knew more. Then we hung up, and I handed the cell phone back to Laurie.

Finally, after a long time had passed, a police officer said, "All right, we can take you down to Penrose now. We've got one of our vans here to transport you."

Shelley Olivier spoke up. "Would you like it if we came with you?" she offered.

"Yes, that would be really nice," I said. Renae volunteered to come, too, for Grace's sake. We all trudged out into the cold and climbed aboard the police van. Gil Datz, an instructor/friend from Laurie's YWAM program, joined us all.

The van was mostly quiet en route, each of us engulfed in our own thoughts. At one point, Gracie looked down at her purple cardigan. "Mom, look," she said. "I've got blood on me. I think it's Rachel's."

I could only nod in response as I reached out to touch her.

"I don't ever want to wash it off," she then said.

"That's okay," I replied. "You don't have to wash it."

Soon we walked through the double doors of the Penrose emergency room. Everything intensified for me in that moment. My husband and my daughter Rachel were being worked on right there in that place. And who knew if Stephanie might be there as well?

New Life's pastor Justin Spicer was waiting for us. He introduced himself as part of the pastoral-care team and asked how he could help us. I hardly knew what to say.

We headed for a side waiting area. A television was going, of course. The sound was annoying. The charge nurse came up almost immediately.

"Are you Marie Works?" she asked.

"Yes."

"It looks like your husband is going to be okay. And they're working on Rachel, too. She's already in surgery; she's in very serious condition. Now I'm wondering, can you give me their official names and dates of birth?" She started writing down the information on her clipboard.

In a minute, I simply had to ask the question that was eating at me.

"Excuse me, but where is Stephanie?"

The nurse hesitated a moment. Then she quietly said, choosing her words carefully, "They didn't bring her here. We don't have her as a patient."

Deep down in my heart I already knew that was the case. When I told my daughters that Stephanie had not been admitted there, it served to move them a notch closer to accepting reality.

Just then the nurse said, "Your husband is about ready to go into surgery. Would you like to come see him?"

"Yes, please."

We walked into the prep room and were relieved to see that David was conscious. I leaned down to give him a kiss. "How are you doing?" I asked.

He smiled as he began explaining what was going to happen in the surgery. "They need to get the lead out of me!" he joked. "Shouldn't take too long."

I was in no frame of mind for humor. I had dreadful news to deliver.

"Honey," I began, trying to loosen the tightness in my throat, "Stephanie didn't make it."

"No, no, she's okay. Rachel's the one in surgery."

"David, I was with her at the last—"

"No, no, no, you're remembering it wrong. Stephanie was on the other side of the van. The guy was shooting from the right side, where Rachel was."

We argued back and forth a little more, and I could tell he wasn't thinking straight. I wanted to tell him something he didn't know, and he wanted to correct what he perceived as my confusion. The tragic facts would have to wait until after his surgery.

Pastor Wanda Moore, a kindly woman who had lost her husband during missionary service in East Africa, was with us, and she led in another prayer. We then said good-bye and retreated to the lobby again.

Police detectives were waiting for an opportune moment to ask us more questions. We went into a side room together, where they wanted to know:

"What direction were the shots coming from?"

"Did you see the shooter?"

"Do you know anyone who would want to do this to you?"

"Could you be connected to this in any way?"

Laurie expressed her opinion that it must have had some tie to the Arvada shootings at YWAM. Generally, we were very subdued during this conversation. We stuck to the facts as we recalled them, without showing emotion. Laurie was hoping the police would offer information in return about what had happened with her twin. But nothing was said.

Then Pastor Justin and a hospital chaplain guided us upstairs to a large surgery waiting room. People from New Life were coming steadily now, bringing food for us. One of Grace's friends arrived.

Cindy Klopfenstein, the mother of Laurie's boyfriend, Jesse, came in and realized we were going to be there for a while. "Would you all like a change of clothes?" she thoughtfully asked.

"Yes, that would be really nice," Laurie replied.

"Okay, let me jot down some sizes," Cindy answered. "I'll see what I can find." She then headed out again.

INTERMISSION

Dr. Ihor Fedorak, the hospital's general trauma surgeon, showed up to see us after awhile. "Let me tell you where things are with Rachel. We're making progress—but we've had to stop the surgery temporarily because her body temperature is dropping. We need to get her back up in a more normal range before we can continue the operation. There's a lot of bleeding to be controlled, and we'll get back to work as soon as we can.

"However, she is alert, she's responding to us, she can nod her head when we ask her questions. So that's good news."

Laurie, Grace, and I thanked him for the update even though it was not all that positive.

Soon word came that David's surgery was finished. "He got through the procedure fine," said Dr. Fisher. "We definitely had to get those bullet fragments out of there. Plus, he actually had a complete bullet still lodged just beneath his navel. One piece of intestine had gotten nicked, and so we repaired that. He's going to be sore for a while, but he'll make it fine."

"Thank you so much, Doctor," I said.

Once David was settled in the recovery room, the girls and I came in. He was in pain, we could tell, and he still wasn't real sharp mentally. We just stood around his bed, patted him, and tried to encourage him.

He looked around at his two daughters. Then came the difficult moment. "Where is Stephanie?" he wanted to know.

I couldn't find the words. He had argued with me the last time, before surgery, about this. I stared at Laurie. His eyes turned to Laurie with a questioning look.

"She's—she's gone," she said in a flat voice.

David stared at us, speechless. His face flooded with despair. He didn't try to debate with us this time. The full force of our family's loss came slamming into his mind. "She's gone?" He dissolved into great sobbing. He even seemed to pass out momentarily from the emotional pain. I leaned over the bed railing to at least hold his hand. It went limp, but I continued to hold it until he regained consciousness.

Finally, he was able to form a new question: "Then what about Rachel? What's going on with her? What have they told you?"

"They were doing surgery on her," I said, "but they had to stop for a while. Something about her body temperature. They said they'll go back in as soon as they can."

By now it was dark outside, somewhere around 5:30 or 6:00. Truthfully, none of us were paying attention to the clock. All of life seemed on hold for the time being.

Soon thereafter, David's brother, John Jr., arrived, having driven down from Denver. A couple of New Life pastors met him at the door and ushered him to a family waiting room at the far end of the ICU hallway. There they updated him on as much as they knew. They also gently broke the news that his niece, Stephanie, had not survived. He broke down and began to cry.

The men eventually walked back up the central hallway—just as David's gurney came heading for his ICU room. I held my breath at this convergence, because the two brothers had not exactly been on friendly terms ever since the Jefferson-Hemings dispute had come into the family. There had also been disagreements over the handling of Gramps's estate.

David looked up, still groggy from the surgery. John came alongside to take his brother's hand. "Hello, David," he said in a gentle voice.

"It's John, Jr. I'm here. I just wanted to let you know I love you." David managed a weak smile, and the two were closer in that moment than they had been for a long time.

We then returned to the waiting area nearby. Laurie's cell phone was going off constantly. I borrowed it from her to go into a small side room with a couple of couches so I could give my parents an update. The confirmed loss of Stephanie was like a sledgehammer to everyone who heard it.

THE VIGIL

Rachel was returned to surgery before long. I prayed fervently that this time would be successful. We kept waiting . . . and waiting . . . and waiting.

Around eight o'clock, Dr. Fedorak came out to see me. I could tell right away by the look on his weary face that things had not gone well. He sat down beside me, composed himself, and then said, "The damage all across her midsection is quite extensive. We've been fighting to stop the bleeding on all the various fronts, but we're not making headway. She continues to deteriorate, and there's not a way to reverse that. "So we've discontinued the surgery again and sent her to the ICU. We're still pumping blood into her, although it appears to be a losing battle. I'm sorry. . . . You and your daughters may go see her now if you like."

"Yes, we will," I said softly. We, along with Jesse, who had arrived a few hours before, made our way to the room. Grace at the last minute held back, not wanting to see her big sister in a desperate state. I allowed her to wait in the hall, and Jesse stayed with her. Laurie entered, along with Pastors Ross Parsley, Rob Brendle, and Lance Coles.

I knew how Grace was feeling, because I was in nearly the same state myself. I didn't think I could bear to see a second daughter on the edge of death this day. But I knew I must go in. I needed to bring her my love and peace no matter how desperate her condition.

My daughter was hooked up to an intimidating array of machines. Tubes ran everywhere, it seemed. She lay motionless on the bed, unconscious. Her forehead was sweating. Several nurses were working on her at once. "She won't be able to talk to you," one of them advised, "but she can hear you. So go ahead and talk to her."

I gently stroked her cheek and hair, then her lower arm. "I love you," I murmured. I began making up a song about how beautiful she was.

Laurie jumped in at this point with a surprisingly strong voice. "You have to fight, Rachel! You have to step up. Come on, you can do it! I know you can. Don't give up! Be brave, like Eowyn in *Lord of the Rings*." She used a couple of other movie analogies to try to rouse a response.

Soon Laurie began to sing songs such as Josh Groban's "Don't Give Up." She was waging spiritual warfare for her sister. It was, in a sense, a poignant reprise of the way they once sang "Mighty Warrior" as little girls jumping off the hearth back in Montana. Laurie prayed aloud with a determination more powerful than anything I could muster—"O God, give her strength. Do Your will. Stop the bleeding in her body and clot the blood. Put Your hand on the places that are bleeding and stop it. Give her Your life!"

I appreciated my daughter's fervor in trying to pull Rachel back from the brink. But as the minutes passed, I began to feel as if a turnaround was not going to happen. I didn't want Rachel to leave this world feeling that she had somehow not tried hard enough. I leaned close to her ear and said quietly, "Honey, it's okay if you don't want to fight anymore. This isn't your fight anymore. It's up to God now. He will take care of you."

Not long afterward, she left us. Her body simply could not knit back together again. She drew her last breath around 10:15 p.m.

I went back out into the waiting room after that and simply tried to keep breathing. I had no more words to use, no more emotions to vent. I was completely drained and in shock. Laurie and Gracie sat down, hugging each other. I hugged them both while Gracie convulsed in tears. If there was something a good mother should say to her child at a moment such as this, I didn't know what it was. I was thoroughly immobilized.

Eventually I looked at Laurie and said, "We have to go tell Dad, don't we?"

She turned her tear-stained face toward me and replied, "Mom . . . I can't. I just can't do it this time. I can't go in there. You have to tell him."

That was understandable. Laurie had done far more that day than any 18-year-old should have had to attempt, from making the first 9-1-1 call, to telling David about Stephanie, to a dozen other things. I would need to shoulder this load myself.

I slowly walked across the waiting area, through the wide door, and into the ICU. I approached my husband's door. I paused. *Oh, God, give me strength*, I prayed silently.

I entered the room at a snail's pace. David's eyes met mine. I kept walking to the foot of his bed.

My body language gave away the news before I ever said a word.

"Rachel's gone too?" he whimpered as the tears began rolling down his cheeks.

"Yes."

"*How come?* She wasn't that badly injured, was she?"

"They couldn't stop the bleeding."

It was more than we thought we could bear. We had started out that day a happy family of six. Now at day's end, we were down to four. Two of the most precious kids on the planet had been snatched away from us in a heartbeat. We were completely ripped apart and left desolate.

We told each other how much we loved one another, somehow hoping to find strength in our words to carry on. But no words could soothe

the awful pain in our hearts. How could we survive? I came closer so we could join hands and pray, "God, we don't understand any of this . . ."

SONG IN THE NIGHT

I (David) stared at the wall after Marie left my ICU room around 11 o'clock to spend the night on the next floor up, where the hospital had graciously set aside a room for her use. Laurie and Grace were only too eager to get out of the hospital altogether and go to the Klopfenstein home. Now I was all by myself.

I tried to calm my mind. I closed my eyes. A song came floating up into my consciousness—a heavy German song I had once learned from the Taizé Community, a retreat center in west-central France. It was based on what the disciple Peter said after a huge disappointment in Jesus' teaching had caused the loss of many followers (John 6:53-68). It was in a minor key, almost like a repetitive dirge:

Herr, wohin, wohin sollen wir gehen?
Du hast Worte ewigen Lebens.

"Lord, where should we go?
You have the words of eternal life."

As I hummed the song again and again, it reflected my feeling exactly. *Lord, I don't understand You at all right now. I don't get it. How could we lose two kids in one day? You're not making any sense. But somehow, I trust You in this situation. Obviously I don't have any better ideas. I'm not going anywhere. I will stick with You, Lord, because You have the words of eternal life. I need You tonight more than ever.*

I kept repeating the song, letting it burrow into my spirit. Eventually I fell asleep.

WHAT NOW?

I don't know how many times I (David) awakened, got back to sleep, and awakened again during that first night. All sense of time escaped me. The drugs I was receiving made it hard even to keep track of day versus night. One time I thought I had been asleep for four or five hours, only to find it had been just five minutes.

I'd never been hospitalized before. I had never experienced so many tubes, needles, probes, and people in white uniforms invading my private space. I was thoroughly overwhelmed. That is why I kept closing my eyes. I couldn't muster the will to cope with all the complexity around me.

Sometime around nine that Monday morning (at least that's what the clock said), Marie reappeared at my bedside. It felt good to see her face once again, even in my foggy condition. I couldn't reach out and hug her, though, for all the equipment in the way.

"Hi," I said. "How are you?"

"Well, I got some sleep," she answered. "They gave me Xanax before I went to bed, which really helped."

"Where are the girls?" I asked. That familiar phrase at our house— "the girls"—now had a starkly different definition. It signified Laurie and Grace, period. That's all.

"They spent the night with the Klopfensteins."

We just looked at each other for a while. Neither one of us knew quite where to begin, what to say, how to go on. Finally I asked, "What are we going to do? What's become of us? How are we going to keep functioning?"

"I don't know . . ."

Dark questions began nibbling around the edges of my brain. *Is our family even going to survive? What if one of us just completely flips out over this?* I studied Marie's face for any sign of meltdown. She seemed to be holding steady.

We began to talk about how the future was going to be radically different from the past—and radically different from the future we had been anticipating. Not that we were afraid of change or risk. When you send your kid on a mission trip, you know in the back of your mind that surprises might pop up. It's "the cost of doing business." You prepare yourself for accidents. Rachel had even landed in a Brazilian hospital that one time.

But never in our worst nightmares did we foresee two of our own getting shot to death in the parking lot of the church we loved. This was absolutely crazy. It certainly didn't fit the plan we thought God had for us.

"Honey, I really thought I knew what God was doing with us. Obviously we're going down a road we hadn't counted on. Did you have any inkling this was going to happen?"

She shook her head.

"I really don't get this. And I really don't like this. I don't know what to say other than I was obviously very wrong about our future."

We reached out to take each other's hands and tried to breathe normally. There wasn't a great deal more to say for now.

First Checkup

Dr. Fisher came by soon. "Hello, David," he greeted me. "Let's see how you're doing today." He began checking the two tubes that came out from the sides of my abdomen, emerging from under a big gauze pad taped to my skin. There was a third tube that came out from another pad on my upper leg.

"This is a wound vacuum system," he explained. "What we do is pack the holes with fairly hard foam to keep everything in place, and then we suction out the bad stuff so the body can get busy healing faster. That's the sound of the machine you hear; it's constantly suctioning the wounds."

I asked questions because I was curious about the technology of how this worked. I also wanted to know what had happened in surgery.

"Well," Dr. Fisher explained, "we found the one bullet right here beneath your navel. It was good to get that out of you—at least most of it. There are still tiny pieces of shrapnel here and there; they won't bother anything. But you'll always see them on an X-ray.

"Now the bullet that hit you in the top of the groin really broke up into lots of pieces. It didn't hit you cleanly; I'm guessing it may have gone through the car door first. Even so, it blew off a chunk of flesh about the size of your fist. That's also the one that hit your small intestine. Had that not gone through the car door and had hit you cleanly—well, that likely would have been fatal, as your femoral artery is right there.

"Anyway, we got you cleaned out as best we could. You're going to be all right."

He also wanted to check my toes to see if I could still feel them, which would mean the blood was circulating properly. He examined the nose tube that was keeping my stomach empty, then the catheter, and he read the vital signs on my chart. All in all, he seemed pleased.

"How will you know if I'm making progress and getting better?" I asked. "What do I have to do?"

"Mainly, prevent infection," he replied. "As we do that, the body can really go to work putting itself back together again." With that, he was on his way.

It wasn't long afterward that my sister, Linnaea, walked in, having flown in from Utah.

"Well, I guess it was a little worse than I told you over the phone, huh?" I was able to say.

"Oh, Dave, I am so, so sorry."

"I just can't believe my Stephanie and Rachel are gone!"

We cried together for a few minutes. Then she said, "Dave, I am here to take care of anything you guys need." This was easy to believe; we had worked well as a team taking care of Gramps in his final months. I had handled financial and logistical issues, while she attended to personal details, even caring for him at his home for a while. I knew she would do the same now.

She turned to Marie. "Tell me what you need," she said. "I'm here to help you any way I can."

"Well, I don't really know," Marie said. "I'm still in a daze."

Linnaea has always been a well-organized, take-charge kind of person, a typical firstborn. "Okay, do you need to make some phone calls? Let's start making a list of people." She whipped out a pad from her purse.

"And how about Laurie and Gracie? Where are they? Who's taking care of them?"

Within the next few minutes she was on to inquiring about Marie's family and their travel plans, as well as my job and what contacts should be made. "And what about things from your apartment? Should we be planning a run up to Denver for clothes? Are there any documents you need?"

Soon the two women were out the door to tackle their lists and make more plans so I could get more rest. I didn't mind my wife being gone for errands such as this; I was fine by myself without a lot of commotion. I had a nearby button I could push whenever the pain got too strong, giving me a new surge of morphine or whatever the amazing juice in the tube was. I also had the comfort of something that might seem juvenile, only it wasn't: a soft teddy bear provided by the hospital. They knew, apparently, that even grown-ups can use something to cuddle. I would tuck it up on my right shoulder and lean my head against it. I'm not too proud to say it felt very good.

Sometime in the afternoon, a nurse stuck her head in the doorway to say, "Two people are here from First Data Corporation—your boss and someone else. Do you want to see them, or shall we turn them away? This is the ICU, after all."

"No, that's okay. They've driven all the way down from Denver. Let them in," I said, knowing that Linnaea had already been in contact with them.

We had a pleasant conversation. "What can we do to take care of you and your family?" my boss, Jill, asked me. She was the one who had hired me in the beginning. She introduced the corporate security officer, a woman with Secret Service background. Jill then started outlining some of the helpful things they had in mind, including a benefit fund they were setting up for contributions from the 29,000 employees all across the company, from Omaha to Singapore.

"Don't worry about recovery time—you take as long as you need," she said with a smile. "The rest of the department team will find a way to cover your projects until you get back."

"Thanks, Jill. I really appreciate that."

A Young Man Named Matthew

By now I was feeling coherent enough to turn on the television and watch some of the news coverage of what had happened to us. Here for the first time I learned the shooter's name: Matthew Murray. Never heard of him. He was 24 years old, they said. His father was a prominent neurologist in the south Denver suburb of Lone Tree. My goodness, we drove within a mile of his office every Sunday on the way to church.

And yes, this guy was the same person who had shot up the YWAM base in Arvada the night before. In fact, he had a history with YWAM. *Boy, this is really strange*, I said to myself. He had been enrolled there back in 2002 for a Discipleship Training School—the same course Laurie had taken, only at a different location. But the leaders had turned him down when it was time to go overseas on a field assignment. They felt there were issues that disqualified him. Matthew took deep offense at this and considered it a personal rejection.

So he had a Christian background? But now they were saying that he posted really dark and violent things on Internet Web sites. In his car, the cops found a copy of *I Had to Say Something*, the recent book by Mike Jones, the male escort who had blown the whistle on Pastor Ted Haggard. That may explain why Matthew had shown up at New Life Church with everything from a Bushmaster assault rifle to two semiautomatic pistols.

"Look, fella," I blurted out, since no one else was in the room just then to hear me, "if you've got a beef with someone, call them out in the street at high noon and have a showdown with them! Don't take it out on me and my girls—you've never even met us. Don't be such a coward!"

I couldn't take any more. I clicked off the TV and lay there in the bed thinking, *If only* . . .

If only I had seen him coming with a little more notice, could I have jumped out and tackled him? That would have been my nature, even if such a move would have been foolhardy. Anything to defend my family.

If only we'd gotten inside the van 30 seconds earlier and had the engine running, so we could have sped away.

If only I'd had my own 12-gauge shotgun that I used for hunting pheasants, so I could have fought back. Nah, he would have had me totally outpowered.

None of this mattered now. We had been caught absolutely helpless. The damage was done, and it was huge. The only thing I could change at this point was how I felt about Matthew Murray. What he had done to us was ghastly. And he was dead now; there would be no arrest, no trial, no judgment against him in this life—and certainly no apology. Would I go through the rest of my life hating him anyway?

I thought about how much God had forgiven me. Granted, I wasn't a murderer like Matthew. But I had a "rap sheet" of my own in heaven, no doubt. I'd lived a fairly colorful life, shall we say, before my conversion experience at age 28. And God had chosen to release me from what I deserved. He had shown me grace instead of condemnation.

Could I do the same for this young man? I somehow knew that was what God was asking.

FIRST TSUNAMI

The New Life pastors had brought in a counselor, Dr. H. Norman Wright, that day, who had warned me that grief was a tide that would rise and fall over time. "Sometime you may be hit with a wave that literally overwhelms you. Be assured that this is not abnormal. It will pass in a few minutes."

I soon found out what he was talking about. Sometime that Monday afternoon, the nursing staff from the emergency room came in to speak with me. They wanted me to know how they had done all they could for Rachel. I started thanking them, and a tsunami began building within me. I had cried before, of course—but this was a deep anguish that threatened to drown me. I gasped; in fact, I started wailing at the top of my voice. *Aaaauugh! Aaaaauugh! Aaaaaauugh!* ICU nurses came running to see what was wrong. Once they realized it was not a physical emergency but rather a grief spasm, they respectfully pulled back. The ER staff also gracefully exited.

I sobbed and groaned out my utter despair. My daughters were gone—cut down in the prime of life, right before my eyes! I began to wretch as I screamed. All of this multiplied the pain in my abdomen, as my diaphragm bolted up and down like a trampoline. It was excruciating throughout the surgery areas, and I was helpless to stop. I was totally out of control.

I carried on like this for probably four or five minutes, shrieking until my voice was hoarse and my whole body wracked with pain. I didn't care what people thought. I just let my emotions rip. In a bizarre sort of way, it felt almost good. And then, I wore myself out. I quieted down from sheer exhaustion. In fact, I fell asleep.

When I awakened later, I was embarrassed. "I'm sorry for what happened," I said to the first nurse who came into my room. "I wasn't mad at you guys or anything. I just . . . reacted, I guess."

"That's all right," she replied. "We fully understand. No need to apologize. In fact, it was probably good for you to let it out that way."

SECOND NIGHT

By evening, Marie was back, along with members of her family who had arrived from Nebraska. Her twin, Mark, and his wife were there, as well as three other brothers and two sisters. It was good to see her parents as well, Russell and Thelma Schaepe.

Laurie came into the room at one point, but not Grace; she had begged off from making the visit. I knew that for the girls, hospitals were just about their least favorite places on earth. They cared about me, and we talked on the phone several times a day. But sitting at my bedside for hours on end was hard for them to endure. Rachel had been in the hospital once before, and then there was the long ordeal of their Gramps. Too many bad memories.

Laurie was getting barraged with cell phone calls from both relatives and family friends all over the country. She found herself serving as informal spokesperson for us all. We talked that evening about how to handle the media reporters, who were everywhere, it seemed—in the hospital waiting room, outside our Denver apartment, at my brother's house, you name it.

"Dad, I'm thinking of giving a statement to the press," Laurie said. "I'm going to write out what to say."

"Oh, no, no, no—I'll take care of that. I know how to deal with reporters, after what all I did back at Monticello," I answered. This was totally irrational—I couldn't even walk yet. The strong painkillers I was receiving made me think I could do more than was possible.

"Are you sure?" my daughter asked with healthy skepticism.

"Sure. I can handle the media—no problem."

Well, nothing actually developed on this front, since the media couldn't exactly walk into my room and shove a microphone in my face. It was Pastor Rob Brendle who the next day sat down beside my bed and gave me a little heart-to-heart advice. "David, you really don't need to say anything to the press. This is not the time for that kind of thing."

At first I was mildly offended. But I had to admit that I could hardly keep track of my own life at the moment. I sure wasn't going to be able to reel off the quick sound bites I imagined, as I had in earlier times.

As Monday came to an end and the room got quiet, Marie and I looked at each other once again. "Well, we made it through one day," I said pensively.

"Yes, we did."

"I'm glad you're able to stay so close. I'd really like it if you were here in my room at night, but you wouldn't get any sleep, what with the traffic in and out," I said. "Still, the hospital is really nice to give you a place. They obviously don't do that for every family."

"Yes, they're really looking out for us."

"What are you going to do when you go upstairs?" I asked.

"Probably take a shower. Just try to wind down. They've got this one channel on the TV that plays just worship music—did you know that?"

"No, I didn't." She proceeded to show me where it was on the Catholic hospital's in-house system.

We eventually kissed each other good night, and I settled down to sleep. *Let your body heal itself,* the surgeon had said. I so much wanted that to happen.

The shift nurse stopped by. On a whiteboard near the door, she wrote her name—a standard practice to help patients know their care-givers. I watched as she penned the letters:

S – T – E – P – H – A – N – I – E

"No, no, no!" I protested. "That just isn't going to work for me." She looked at me quizzically. "My daughter—we lost her yesterday—" I broke down trying to finish the sentence.

"Oh, I'm so sorry!" she replied as she quickly erased the whiteboard. She had heard about our tragedy but hadn't made the name connection.

I regained my composure enough to ask, "What's your middle name?"

"Amanda," she answered.

"Okay. Can I call you that instead?"

"Absolutely," she replied, writing it on the board.

She then finished preparing the room for overnight, checked my IV one last time, made sure my call button was accessible, and dimmed the lights. Soon I was alone once more.

I slept well for a couple of hours, then woke up. It was hard to get comfortable. I slept again, then half-awakened sometime after one o'clock in the morning. I was drowsy, but at the same time, I was conscious enough to think of a song by New Life's Desperation Band, "Maker of Heaven." It talked about God "making all things new again" and also included a prayer—"Take over my life; I surrender now."

Pretty soon I was humming the song. After a short while I switched to a second Desperation Band song, "I'm Coming Your Way." I started singing out loud:

If all we have is love, then all I have is You;
If life is what we choose, then I choose You.
I'm coming Your way,
I'm coming Your way. . . .[5]

I felt a light touch on my hand. I opened my eyes to see "Amanda" standing by my bed. She looked down at me with kindness. "I heard you singing," she said.

"Yes. It's a song I sing with my family sometimes."

"What's it about?"

"It's about trusting God when you don't have anything left. I guess I'm understanding that I can still go on. I can go on with life." I started to choke up.

She kept waiting to see if I would say any more. I continued, "Sometimes I don't feel like going on. But I can. I can do this."

"Yes, you can," Amanda replied. "You really can."

With that, I closed my eyes again. Soon I was back to sleep. The next time I woke up, two hours had passed, and she was out at her workstation again. Tuesday was already underway.

BEYOND VICTIMHOOD

Marie arrived in my room the next morning hardly functional. She had been given more Xanax for sleeping than she apparently needed. It was hard for her to track with a conversation.

Fortunately, Linnaea and other family members were ready and eager to handle things Marie could not. Her brother Dan and sister Alesia, for example, volunteered to take Marie to Denver to get things we needed from the apartment. Dan would drive my truck back to Colorado Springs so Marie would have something to drive.

As for me, I was still receiving little more than ice chips by mouth. Not that I was hungry at all. My digestive system was thoroughly messed up.

My brain was working a little better, however. As I lay there in my bed, I remembered something I had learned nearly two years before in a seminar on overcoming trauma. A number of us Thomas Jefferson descendants had gone to a helpful conference at Eastern Mennonite University (only an hour's drive from Monticello) called "Coming to the Table." The professor had shown a diagram of two interlocking circles (see appendix) to portray victimhood and violence. One side represented the victim or survivor; the other side represented the aggressor or enemy.

But they overlapped. "A victim/survivor," said the professor, "if he or she does not deal with things that have happened in the trauma—be it slavery or any other trauma—can turn into the aggressor. The victimized can become the victimizer. Another way to say this is 'Hurt people hurt people.'

"None of us want this to happen. So let's talk about how to break the cycle." Out came a second diagram that looked like a snail on its side (again, see appendix). "You can keep going around and around the same core of your trauma—or you can break away into new territory. You can bog down in repetitions of sadness, resentment, and aggravation—or you can accept the loss and move on. You can *choose to live*."

I lay there that Tuesday morning reviewing this instruction. It became clear to me that I could stay in my circle of shock and fear—or I could break free. I didn't have to become mired in bitterness and anger and reprisal fantasies. I could move to higher spiritual ground.

I need to share this with Marie and the girls, I told myself. *But only when the time is right.*

STEP BY STEP

By Wednesday, December 12, it was time for me to migrate out of the ICU to a regular hospital room. I was glad for the progress this represented, although I didn't look forward to giving up my "pain juice" button. Now I would have to ask a nurse for relief medication if I needed it.

Somewhere about this time, Marie and I came to clarity on a move of far greater proportions. We needed to get out of the Denver apartment once and for all. The thought of going back to that noise and commotion and sirens and drug deals going down—no way. Our nerves were shot. We simply wouldn't be able to handle it.

So the next time Pastor Justin Spicer said, "What can I do to help you?" we answered, "Well, if you're really serious about that—you could find us a new place to live!"

He didn't blink. "Okay. What do you have in mind?"

"We'd actually love to move here to Colorado Springs," I said, as Marie nodded. "I'm pretty sure I could talk to my company and get permission to work remote from home. That's happening all across the IT world these days. I could drive up to Denver a day a week or so to be in the office. But most of what I do is online anyway. And that way we'd be close to the church and all of you."

In saying this, I conveyed our undiluted love and appreciation for New Life Church. They were being absolutely wonderful to us. A few outsiders said to us later on, "How could you go back to the church where such an awful thing happened to you?"

Our thinking was 180 degrees opposite of that; how could we *not* go back to the church that loved us, helped us, and meant so much to our whole family?

"What kind of place would you be interested in?" Pastor Justin asked.

"Well, considering my present state," I replied, looking down at my right leg, "it would be nice if it had a master bedroom and an office on the same floor, so I wouldn't have to climb stairs."

"And two other bedrooms," Marie added. "Laurie and Grace have certainly paid their dues when it comes to room-sharing. They need their own spaces now."

"What about a patio home so I wouldn't have to do outside maintenance?" I said.

"That makes sense," the young pastor answered.

"What would really be neat would be a gated community, for the sake of security," I added. "If we didn't have to worry about some stranger coming right up to our front door, we'd rest easier. Does Colorado Springs have any place like that where we could just rent for a while?"

"Yes, I think so. We have some real-estate people in the church. I'll see what I can find out."

UPSIDE DOWN

A far more sobering topic to discuss with Pastor Justin was the girls' memorial service. We couldn't set a date because we didn't know how long I would be hospitalized. But we needed to start putting the service together.

He brought along his colleague, Pastor Mel Waters, who carries the main responsibility at New Life for funeral planning. Pastor Mel had a checklist of all the details to think about, and Marie brought out some notes she had been jotting on the subject.

"Last night before I went to sleep, I finally got some inspiration," she said. "Here are some songs I'd like to have in the service." She began naming them, and then added, "How about if we have Jessie Gingrich sing 'Everlasting God'? I feel it would be good both for her and for us. Pastor Ross and the worship team can do the other songs. I haven't thought out exactly in what order."

"That's okay; there's time to get that worked out," Pastor Mel assured us.

"Then I'd like to have some of the girls' friends speak about what they meant to them. For example, Connie Schertel will probably come from Montana. She should speak about Stephanie. For Rachel, I was thinking about having Aimee Donahue, her YWAM friend, for sure. And then possibly J. T. Weatherford, if he's agreeable."

Pastor Mel kept writing notes.

In a way, this was all very backward. Kids—usually grown-up kids—are supposed to plan the funerals of their parents, not the other way around. Of all the hard things that can happen in a person's life, the hardest has to be burying your own child—let alone two of them.

But in another sense, we actually felt good about being able to pay tribute to our daughters and honor them before a large gathering. It was another way to do something for Stephanie and Rachel. We looked forward to God giving us the grace to handle the occasion.

By the time we ended the conversation that day, we didn't have everything nailed down, of course. But we had at least settled that we would have a private burial ahead of the public service at church, and the main components of the service were coming together.

My sister, Linnaea, had meanwhile been out scouting cemeteries.

Obviously, we had not expected to need one anytime soon in our lives, especially not in Colorado Springs. She brought us pictures and data sheets on the various options.

We ended up choosing the small, rustic cemetery up north in the village of Monument. Suffice it to say, it is not Forest Lawn. The terrain is bumpy, the grass is what manages to grow on its own in this arid climate, the headstone rows are a bit random, and the boundary is marked by a chain-link fence. It's a no-frills, country sort of place—what the girls would have called authentic.

The view, however, is priceless. When you raise your attention from the hit-or-miss groundskeeping, you see majestic Pikes Peak soaring to its snowy 14,110-foot summit in the distance. The brilliant blue of the Colorado sky and the sweep of the plateau leading up to the mountains make you think of the classic words of Psalm 121:

> I lift up my eyes to the hills—
> where does my help come from?
> My help comes from the LORD,
> the Maker of heaven and earth.
> He will not let your foot slip—
> he who watches over you will not slumber. (verses 1-3)

Here we would lay our girls to rest. Living nearby, we could come here often. So could many of our new friends. Here, the God of solace and peace would help us all find comfort.

FALTERING FORWARD

By that Wednesday afternoon, the flow of visitors was starting to pick up, now that I was more accessible. The hospital tried to conceal my presence by listing me under a pseudonym, but that was only partly effective. One of the first to arrive was my brother, John, from Denver. He wished me well in my recovery. On this visit, we stayed away from touchy subjects of the past, concentrating on the present. He said he was thinking of setting up a public memorial fund in honor of the girls, and I told him that would be all right with us.

Other visitors began to show up after learning by word of mouth what room I was in—people from the church as well as Denver friends. It was good to see them all. Marie and I genuinely appreciated their concern.

But I found that visiting with people quickly wore me out. I had no endurance, it seemed. The doctor had warned me to be careful about that, because I had pumped out every last drop of adrenaline I had, and my reserves were depleted.

Marie and my sister began noticing a pattern: Whenever I was running out of gas, I would begin to yawn. From that point on, I would last no more than five minutes! I would go out like a light, sound asleep, regardless of who was in the room. My yawning became their signal to say to guests, "Well, thanks so much for stopping by. It's been nice to visit with you."

A nurse supervisor named Cheri decided to clamp down on the traffic before it got me to the edge. She set up a restriction on how many visitors I could receive (maximum three at a time) and how long they could stay (no more than 15 minutes). The only exceptions were immediate family and the pastors from New Life. She was tough about it, but her action was no doubt appropriate.

She and the other staff wanted me to save some of my steam for a goal of their own: walking. I started out by getting up to go to the bathroom, and followed that with the joy of taking a shower. Then came Thursday morning, when a nurse walked in bright and early to say, "Okay, let's go out in the hall."

I wasn't thrilled with this idea. I tried to tell her I'd only had Jell-O and broth till now. She would not be dissuaded. She coaxed me out into the corridor and loaded my various paraphernalia—the IV, the vacuum pump, and so on—into a wheelchair. "Here, you can push this and hold on to the handles for balance." In other words, no more pampering.

"Let's see you go 50 feet and then come back," she said. "Walk down to that corner and then turn around. You can do it!"

I asked for a pillow to prop over the wheelchair back so I could push my belly into it for relief. Then I started shuffling down the corridor. I was definitely shaky. But I didn't collapse after all. I managed to reach the corner.

Why stop now? I said to myself. I was somehow feeling stronger. I decided to keep going. I ended up taking a full lap around the floor of this high-rise hospital. Instead of doing a hundred feet, it was more like a hundred yards. I was proud of myself.

"Go! Go! Go!" said Cheri when she saw me. She kept pushing me to walk, so much that I affectionately named her "the Nazi." I obeyed her to the point of doing two full laps a day, morning and evening. And before long, as I got more broth and Jell-O inside of me, I ditched the wheelchair and simply held on to the hall railing instead.

On one of these walks, however, a grief spasm hit me without warning. I still can't say what triggered it. I was just walking along when I suddenly broke up. I began to convulse in tears over Stephanie and Rachel. I could only stand there gripping the railing as I sobbed. The nurse let me work it through and then gently guided me through the rest of the walk and back to my room.

These eruptions happened four or five times during my hospital stay. I learned not to fear them. The psychological and emotional release—and even the physical release—was incredible. I actually came to laugh at the end of them, they felt so good. They were a necessary part of my healing.

In calmer moments, I turned on my laptop computer, which Linnaea had brought to me. I sat in the room recliner and began e-mailing friends and work associates. I thought it would help them simply to hear from me, even if the message was short.

When I got my cell phone back, I called a few people just to let them hear my voice. They said they really appreciated this. On Thursday, I called in to the weekly First Data teleconference between the Denver and Omaha teams. "Hi, everybody," I said. "Just wanted you all to know that I'm here and going to be okay!"

"David, it's really great to hear your voice," they responded. "We're all thinking about you."

I didn't stay on the line for the full meeting; I couldn't make myself concentrate that long. But the contact with old friends and associates felt good.

I got another connection to the outside world when one of the pastors brought me a DVD of New Life's special "Family Meeting" held on Wednesday night. Senior Pastor Brady Boyd felt it was a good idea to bring the whole congregation together and talk about what had happened. In preparation for this, the church had quickly replaced every shot-up window and patched every bullet hole in the drywall to give people a sense of normalcy the minute they walked through the doors. What the workers accomplished in 72 hours was impressive.

The Desperation Band led the worship that night, backed up by the 90-voice choir. Pastor Brady then stood up to say in his opening paragraph, "We are making a declaration here tonight: *We will not be governed by fear.*" That line, understandably, became the local headline the next morning. But when he went on to specifically mention Stephanie and Rachel, his voice broke. He couldn't say another word for more than 20 seconds. He was feeling what we were feeling, and it meant the world to us.

Colorado's Lieutenant Governor Barbara O'Brien was there to convey her condolences, as well as state Attorney General John Suthers and Colorado Springs Mayor Lionel Rivera. U.S. Senator Wayne

Allard sent a video from Washington. It was good to know that people far and near had us in their thoughts.

SETBACK

I figured that by the weekend, I'd be doing really well. The only trouble was, I somehow got my sleep cycle off track, lying awake at night and dozing throughout the day. My digestive system couldn't seem to get back into gear with solid food. I was terribly nauseated.

My abdomen was in no shape for more distress than it had already endured. The first time I had to vomit, I was scared to death that I'd rip everything apart. The same was true when I had to cough. I would press in on my midsection—which was excruciating—and then go ahead. Amazingly, neither vomiting nor coughing caused any damage. But I felt really lousy.

I prayed for some kind of improvement, some lift from God. He seemed totally silent. This was most distressing of all. He had always been there. Where was He now? This was the hardest ordeal I had ever gone through, and He seemed a million miles away. Why? Had I done something wrong? It was bad enough to lose the girls, then to realize how mistaken we had been about our family's future. But without God's presence, how could I possibly go on? For some reason, He hadn't protected us in the parking lot. I became deeply discouraged.

Meanwhile, the rest of the world was patiently waiting for us to set a firm date for the girls' memorial service, which depended upon my being able to attend. Out-of-town family members were waiting in hotels; the media kept asking questions; the church needed to know how to plan. They had already canceled the remaining performances of *Wonderland*, in fact, out of respect for us. "This is a time to mourn, not a time to celebrate," Pastor Brady had said.

So when would I get out of the hospital? It all seemed murky.

Finally, I said to Marie and Linnaea, "Go ahead and nail down the service for Wednesday afternoon [December 19]—whether I'm there or not. We can't stall any longer, with Christmas coming and everything. I would feel terrible not to be present, but we can't keep everyone else hanging." Still, the thought of my daughters' bodies actually being buried without me seeing them tore me up.

My wife and sister were busy trying to answer questions and handle details. Mark, Marie's twin, had made a trip to Denver to get my suit for the service as well as pick up other needed items. Another brother-in-law, Andy, with his wife, Rose, took charge of ordering flowers. Still another brother-in-law, Joe, was helping to keep the young nieces and nephews happy as they waited, since his grown boys weren't with him. Mark took our Gracie bowling on Saturday, where they met up with Andy and his family.

Marie, meanwhile, carried the additional concern of her 78-year-old father, who had landed in another room of the same hospital not long after getting off the plane from Nebraska. He has chronic lung limitations, and in our rarified air (6,000-foot altitude), he couldn't get his breath. Doctors were working to stabilize him.

One night that weekend, Marie went to bed, tossed and turned for a time, but still couldn't get to sleep. Frustrated, she got up and decided to go to her dad's room. He was still awake. The two of them began talking about what had befallen them, and how this whole tragedy was pulling the Schaepe side of the family together like never before.

Marie leaned against her father's shoulder and began to weep. In that moment she didn't have to keep being the strong adult in the storm. She could let down and just be her daddy's daughter for once. "I love you, Dad," she said. He gave her a warm response. It was a healthy release for her.

Sunday came—a full week since the tragedy. I still wasn't feeling good at all. I managed to stay awake to watch, with Marie, an online church service on my computer that morning. The nausea still tormented me.

Soon after lunchtime, two special visitors—Nancy Gallegos and her husband—arrived to bring me a gift of live music. The elevator doors opened, and out they came with a full-size harp! Such things are not easy to cart around, but there they were with smiles on their faces. "David, we came to encourage you today," they said.

Nancy set up her instrument out by the nurses' station, and I was wheeled out in my recliner. She must have played for an hour—"Great Is Thy Faithfulness," "Agnus Dei," Jared Anderson's song "Amazed." Soon other patients were coming out of their rooms to get in on the concert.

The music had a calming effect on us all. When she finished, we were totally relaxed. We clapped and thanked her profusely. What a special gift was ours that afternoon.

FAREWELL TO NEVERLAND

Then it was back to the room. A week ago that very hour, I had been in one surgery suite, Rachel in another. It felt like a century ago. And yet, I hadn't moved very far. I was still under the same roof as back then.

Around three o'clock, Linnaea commented to me, "You know, David, you always seem to keep the lights down low in this room. And you speak very softly. You play your music very low. Everything's really subdued. Is that the way you want it to be? It seems like you're trying to reduce the sensory input as low as possible."

I opened my eyes and looked around. She was right. I was consistently limiting the outside stimuli.

"I guess you're right," I said to my sister. "I hadn't noticed."

"At the same time, your sense of smell is incredible. You can point out every smell in this room! I only smell 'hospital.'" We talked about whether limiting my visual input had heightened my sense of smell, as apparently happens with some blind people.

I kept thinking about this after she left the room. I remembered what one of the counselors had told me earlier in the week, that it is helpful in processing grief to write things down. "You don't have to be organized or profound," she had said. "Just start putting down whatever comes to mind."

I decided to try it. For the first time in a week I picked up a pen. I pulled out a legal pad and started writing. I intended to list my fears.

> *He's coming after me again. Or someone like him. Or another traumatic situation. How do I stop them? I can't stop them.*

But then as I got going, my words morphed into something much different—a description of how I had normally coped with difficulty.

> *I have a secret place I go when things get bad. It's an imaginary world without properties, size, dimensions. It can be whatever I need it to be.*
>
> *I've been hiding there since Dad and Mom started fighting [back during my childhood]. Now, that [place] has been destroyed. Thoughts are flooding in. I can't stop them. My refuge is destroyed. I've been trying to patch it up, but it isn't working.*
>
> *I don't want to leave my world. I'd have to open my eyes and embrace this moment. And if I do, I will barf, and I will retch, and I will wail, like I wanted to do when I was a little*

*boy. "Neverland" has been burned and pillaged. I'm lost and
can't find my way.*

*I need to open my eyes to this present moment, but I'm
afraid. . . .*

I laid down the pen and meditated on what I had written. I knew
it wasn't a brilliant self-analysis by any means. But it was accurate from
my own personal perspective.

"So what do I do with this, God?" I prayed. "Does this have any
significance?"

In that moment, for the first time in a week I sensed communication with God. I felt as if He were saying to me, *I want to bring you out
of this dark spot. You need to say good-bye to Neverland. Close the door.
Leave that imaginary place. Come with Me."*

"Where are we going?"

I'm taking you into Me.

"What do You mean, Lord?" I countered. "I'm already one of Yours."

I want to take you to a place you've never been before.

"Where's that?"

*Right here—in the present moment. You haven't really seen Me here.
There's a beauty, a completeness, and a richness in the present moment that
you haven't experienced, and I want to show it all to you.*

I lay there pondering what this might mean. "Well, okay, God—
what do You want me to see?" I said.

I need for you to open your eyes.

I followed His instructions. Then God seemed to continue:

*The next person who walks through your door, receive as from Me. And
the next. And the next.*

I wasn't so sure about that. The next person to come in, I said to
myself, would probably be a nurse with a needle wanting to draw more

blood! Or some reporter sneaking in. "God, I don't know that I can do what You're saying."

Silence.

Presently a nurse came in for a routine check on me. She didn't have any needles this time. She just did her job, and before leaving, she added, "God bless you."

A simple word of blessing. There in the present moment.

I decided God's leading wasn't so questionable after all. Maybe I should keep my eyes open more. Another hospital staffer came in, and then a third. Every exchange turned out to be positive.

Whenever I felt nauseated, I would focus on the clock or the black towel dispenser on the wall, instead of closing my attention inward. I kept looking outward. To my surprise, I felt more in control, more uplifted.

At nine o'clock that evening, I received my usual anti-nausea shot, which also had the side effect of making me drowsy. I settled down for a night of sleep. But then—

An hour later I was wide awake. How frustrating. I began to squirm. My mind was racing. If I didn't get this sleep thing straightened out soon, how was I ever going to get back on my feet?

After 15 minutes, I hit the call button. The overnight nurse who responded was named Janet.

"I can't sleep again," I said. "This isn't working. Give me something to knock me out, okay?"

She moved from the foot of my bed up to the side and looked down at me. She thought for a moment. Then she said, in her lovely Jamaican accent, "Mistuh Wukks, I can give you sleeping pills—or you can overcome it right now. What's your choice going to be?"

I was startled. "What did you say?"

She repeated herself. The word *overcome* struck me. We had decided to include a song called "Everyone Overcome" in the memorial service, because we viewed the girls as overcomers. There is no way Janet would have known that. "Mistuh Wukks, you can take sleeping pills, and this process will go on for weeks. Or we can overcome this tonight—right now."

I didn't know what to make of this. "Okay, uh . . . what does 'overcome' look like?" I finally asked.

"We will get you up out of bed," she answered, "and then we will go for a walk. We will walk as long as you want. Then we will come back to the room—and you can do whatever you want—whatever you would do if you were home and couldn't sleep. What would you do there?"

"Oh, I'd probably get up and work on the computer."

"Then you do that here. There's no pressure to sleep. You don't have to do anything. But you can overcome this problem right now."

I got up, and with Janet's help, I walked a lap through the now-empty hallways. The longer I walked, the more my head seemed to clear. When I finally got back to my room, I sat down in the recliner rather than climbing into bed. I started reading. I didn't go back to bed until 11 o'clock.

The next thing I knew, it was 4:00 in the morning. I had slept five hours straight. My first thought upon awakening was *Oh, no, it's not morning yet. I need to get back to sleep.* But then I remembered Janet's words. I told myself, *Wait a minute—I don't have to do anything. I can just lie here and relax. I can meditate on God's goodness in the present moment.*

In fact, I didn't go back to sleep the rest of that night. But I didn't stress about it. By morning, I was feeling very good. I thanked Janet for her wise counsel. I ate a portion of breakfast.

And I was never nauseated again.

OUT THE DOOR

Dr. Fisher showed up around nine o'clock that Monday morning. "So how are you doing?" he asked.

"Good!" I replied. "Really good. I think I've turned a corner—at least physically. I had a very good night, thanks to Janet's advice. She helped me work through a bunch of stuff."

"Glad to hear it," he said. He began checking my incisions. He was pleased with what he found. "You're going in the right direction. Shall we get you out of here today?" he asked.

"Oooh, really?"

"You can take the wound vacuum with you; there's a portable model available. We'll just set you up with a shoulder bag to carry it. And we'll teach you and your wife what you need to do."

"But I don't know if I'm ready emotionally," I said. "What if I have a relapse of some kind? I sure wouldn't want to have to come back in."

"Okay, then let's wait 24 hours," Dr. Fisher replied. "I'll have the staff work on all the exit papers in the meantime, and then when I show up at 9:30 tomorrow morning, out you go."

"Sounds good to me!"

When Linnaea arrived, she was surprised to see the dramatic change in me. "Wow, what's going on?" she asked.

"Hey, I'm doing great!" I told her. "I can get out of here tomorrow!"

That launched her into a new flurry of activity. Soon she and Marie were off to the four winds making arrangements. They reserved a suite at the Residence Inn just across Interquest Parkway from New Life Church, where some of the extended family and friends would be staying through the memorial service. We would spend the rest of the week there. Laurie and Grace would be able to rejoin us, after eight nights at the Klopfenstein home.

Marie, with her sisters Alesia and Sara, stopped by the police department headquarters to see about getting personal things out of the minivan, which had of course been impounded for evidence. But the police were willing to release things like my reading glasses, Stephanie's purse, her Bible, Rachel's Bible, music CDs, and other things we wanted. Marie and her sisters didn't actually see the minivan, which would have been far too traumatic at that early stage; the officers went out into the garage and got the items for them.

The same two sisters took Marie, Laurie, and Grace out shopping to buy clothes for the memorial service. They even picked up things for me to wear.

While the women were out and busy, I did more walking. I felt stronger and stronger. At one point, I came to a door that led to a stairwell. I got an idea. I asked the nurse who was accompanying my walk, "Can I try some stairs?"

She looked at me for a second, saw my eagerness, and then said, "Oh, well—why not?" She probably figured that if it hurt too badly, I would back off.

I started up the staircase. One step . . . second step . . . third step. I could handle it! Halfway up to the next floor, I pulled out my cell phone. "Marie, you're not going to believe where I am right now!" I fairly shouted. "I'm in the middle of going up stairs!"

"You're kidding!" she said.

"No, it's true. I can do this!"

I could tell she wasn't entirely convinced that I was out of the woods. And of course, I wasn't. But we both were glad to be heading toward an open horizon after so much fog.

The actual discharge on Tuesday took longer than expected, because Dr. Fisher got called into an emergency surgery that morning. We ended up sitting around for hours. We could hardly complain, however. After all, he had dropped everything back on December 9 for *my* emergency. We couldn't begrudge his attention to somebody else's crisis.

I used the time to take a shower and finish getting organized to leave. Dr. Fisher showed up, apologetic, right after lunch; he was still in his surgical scrubs. "Still doing okay?" he asked.

"Yes!" I replied.

"Then let's get you out of here. All the paperwork is done, and I'll get the nurses going on the discharge."

After nine days, it was pretty hard to say good-bye to the doctor who had brought me back from the brink. I thanked him as best I could. Not one to have a scene, Dr. Fisher shrugged his shoulders humbly as if it were just another day at the office.

Soon I was being rolled in the mandatory wheelchair toward the doors. I drew in my first whiff of cold winter air and got myself into Linnaea's rental car. I took one last look at Penrose Hospital with a mixture of sadness and gratitude. These people had worked their hearts out for us, and while they had not won every battle, they had given it their best.

TWO ROSES
IN THE SNOW

David's release from the hospital was a big step for the girls and me (Marie). We three had already spent Monday night at the Residence Inn, and now we would be welcoming David as well.

Linnaea picked David up from the hospital. On the way to the hotel, David asked her to swing by the New Life Church parking lot. He wanted to see again the place where everything had broken loose.

"Wow. It's all much closer than I remembered. He was just right there, wasn't he?" David said as he pointed a few yards away. "How did any of us survive?"

After a few minutes, they came on to the hotel and we got David's things settled.

The two-bedroom suite included a kitchen, dining area, and living room. It felt almost like our apartment in Denver. "How do you guys like it?" David asked.

"Dad, this is really nice," Laurie said.

"We have TVs in every room!" Gracie added.

"Isn't it good to be together again?" David said. "I really missed you guys. It wasn't any fun visiting me in the hospital, was it?"

"No!" they both replied.

"Well, Daddy is going to be okay. I've got some healing to do over the next while. Actually, we all have some healing to do. But we can do this. We can do this together. We have a lot of help from our families and from our family at New Life. And most important of all, God is with us." We spent a few moments hugging each other.

What lay ahead for us would be both good and difficult. In just a few hours, we would be heading to the 5:00 p.m. viewing at the funeral home, a place southeast of the downtown area called the Shrine of Remembrance.

I had already been there the day before to do some work ahead of time. I suppose I got more involved in the preparation than some people would find comfortable. But if you stop to think about it from a historical point of view, 100 years ago most funeral preparations happened at home. That is where most people died in the first place, not in a sterile hospital somewhere. That is where the body stayed, right on through the visitation hours. Only at the last moment did families transport their dead loved ones to a church for the public service.

Like a frontier mother, I wanted to make sure my girls looked right. I wanted to work on their hair and arrange the jewelry to match their outfits. In my way of thinking, this was my chance to tell my girls good-bye and say "I love you" one last time. I knew I could have let the mortuary's beautician take care of fixing their appearance; that's what most families do these days. But why couldn't I handle this myself? It would be my last opportunity to do something for my daughters.

Two of my sisters, Sara and Alesia, said they would go with me, along with Pastor Wanda Moore. Pastor Mel Waters met us there, and after a few minutes we were introduced to a mortuary staff person, who led us to the preparation room. "Here is where we will bring the girls on gurneys, one at a time," he explained. "I would suggest that you wait out in the hallway until I come back and let you know we're ready for you."

Alesia and Sara stayed close by my side, in case I would need their support. I was glad to have them along. Inside, however, I was calm and focused on what I had come to do.

The first thing, I told the staff member, was that I wanted some locks of each girl's hair as keepsakes. He brought a pair of scissors and some small envelopes. "How many locks do you want me to cut from each?" he asked.

"Five," I answered. One was for Rachel's friend Aimee, who would be flying in from Virginia for the service. Another would be for Aimee's sister Sarah, who wanted to take it on her upcoming summer mission trip to Africa—Rachel had planned to go too, and so this was a way for a part of her to fulfill that dream. The three other sets were for Laurie, Grace, and myself.

The girls were already dressed in the clothes I had sent ahead for them. Stephanie's outfit was a special *salwar kameez* from East India, a short-sleeved tunic in warm red-orange colors with elaborate gold and bead-embroidered embellishments, plus a pair of ankle-length billowy pants and wrap. Her shoes were actually a pair of Laurie's that she had bought overseas, matching the Indian look perfectly.

I decided to put in her favorite classic earrings, small gold hoops we had bought together at Macy's in Park Meadows Mall. It had been hard work finding just what she wanted, which was something she had seen the lead actress wear in a romantic British film about England's class wars.

Rachel was in a new sleeveless silky blouse that was dusky gray with a navy floral pattern as well as navy accents on the bodice and straps.

She wore her new pair of pencil jeans and her favorite pair of Converse low-top shoes. We had to find a shawl to add, as we needed more coverage for her arms, neck, and just below the neck. We added a pair of earrings given to her by Aimee.

Rachel's hair didn't need a lot of work, because she wore it straight. Stephanie's, which was curly, was a bigger challenge. As I worked with a curling iron, I shed a few tears as I thought about how many times Stephanie and I had gotten frustrated working to bring out the curl in our hair. It was just one of the things mothers and daughters do together, and this was the last time I would ever be able to do her hair.

We asked for some nail polish to apply: a warm orange to match Stephanie's Indian outfit, and Rachel's current favorite, which was black. The funeral home didn't have any black on hand, so Pastor Wanda headed out to buy some.

It took close to 45 minutes to get the girls looking presentable. I finally reached the goal, fulfilling my heart's desire to make my girls look just right. Before leaving the funeral home, we also stopped to check on the pair of old-fashioned pine caskets that David and I had chosen earlier from a catalog Linnaea had brought to us.

When I got back to David after this outing, he said, "I'm really proud of you. I couldn't have done something like that."

"Well, it was a gift I wanted to give," I replied.

A Family United

The winter sun was setting behind the mountains that Tuesday afternoon as the funeral home's stretch limousine pulled up to the hotel to take us to the viewing. Laurie and Grace reminded each other of a previous limo ride they had enjoyed when we celebrated Gramps's 75th birthday with a special dinner. On this occasion, we brightened the atmosphere somewhat by inviting Connie Schertel, Stephanie's close friend from Montana, and her eight-month-old baby daughter, Gloria, to ride with us. The six of us got into the long black car and settled in for the half-hour ride down the freeway.

When we arrived, I (Marie) pushed David's wheelchair through the back door and into the lobby, where everyone was waiting. The director showed our family the way to the chapel, a large room with soft lighting that seated about 150. Flowers covered the front area. David was on his feet by now, while Laurie and Grace followed us, holding each other closely. This was the moment we had dreaded but also wanted. Here we would be a family together one more time.

In the center of the room on an easel was a huge color photo, three feet wide by four feet tall, of Stephanie and Rachel smiling. It had been taken on a bus in Hong Kong near the end of the China mission trip the previous summer. Rachel had taken it herself, stretching out her left arm to aim the camera. Now Laurie had managed to snag the photo off Rachel's Facebook page, and the funeral home had gotten it enlarged as a centerpiece for the viewing and memorial service.

We looked at the photo, and our common reaction was that the girls seemed incredibly real. We almost wanted to say, "Hi, guys!" Their vibrant energy just radiated.

We then moved to the right, where Rachel's casket awaited. There she lay, still and somber. Her trademark blue eyes were inaccessible now. The promise ring we'd given her when she turned 13, a sign of her pledge to save herself for marriage, was no longer on her finger; it had been cut off in the emergency room before surgery. She was out of reach, and our throats tightened at the harsh reality.

We placed inside the casket her latest journal in progress, as well as her favorite stuffed animals; these would go to the grave with her. We then turned to Stephanie's casket on the left, where we placed her special teapot. Again, we felt a pervasive emptiness. This was not our first-born child. This was only a shell. The real Stephanie had left this world.

David was the first to speak. He cleared his throat as he looked at Laurie, Grace, and me. "They're not here," he simply said. "This isn't them."

We nodded in agreement as Laurie said, "You're right, Dad." To all of us, the picture in the middle was what was real. We knew they were still alive, only in a much better place. That place was far away from us for now. But we would see them again, and when we did, they would be just as effervescent and wonderful as we had always known them to be. We gained great comfort in the words of the Apostles' Creed, "I believe in . . . the communion of saints . . ." David and I drew Laurie and Grace to us and held each other close while we looked at the open caskets.

Some 10 minutes went by before we signaled to the funeral director that he could open the doors for the rest of the crowd. In came the family members—all of my eight siblings except one brother (who was in Iraq), their spouses, their kids, my grieving parents, Linnaea and her family, and David's mother and her husband, who had just flown in from Kansas City. His mother's health was not strong, and on this occasion she could hardly speak. She could only weep over her two grandchildren, snatched away so inexplicably at such young ages. Stephanie had been e-mailing her in recent months trying to collect family history. Now that dialogue had been abruptly cut off.

At least four New Life pastors were present as well as close friends from the church. A cluster of young people from theMILL gathered around Laurie. The out-of-town friends numbered at least a dozen, which was amazing in light of their having to book last-minute flights in the thick of the Christmas travel crunch.

They circulated by one casket and then the other. We sat waiting on the front row, David in the center aisle in his wheelchair. One by one they came by with reddened eyes to shake our hands and murmur words of condolence. Some people, we noticed, could not even bear to approach the caskets. That was all right; we knew their hearts were with us regardless.

When most had paid their respects, Pastor Mel stood up to address the group. "Thank you so much for coming tonight," he said. "I understand that most of you are family and close friends. Some of you have come from out of town to be here. On behalf of David and Marie and their family, I want to thank you for being here this evening. I know it means a lot to them. This is a difficult time for all of us. But it is good to have family and friends close by to help us through these times. . . . David, is there anything you'd like to add?"

My husband lifted himself out of his wheelchair at this point to say, "Yes, it is good to see you all here. We appreciate and love every one of you. Tomorrow, the service is at two o'clock at New Life. You'll see me being wheeled in then, even though obviously I can stand. The trouble is, I don't have much energy yet, so the wheelchair is a better choice for now." He gave a bit of explanation about his wounds and his ongoing recovery. "If you'd like to continue to view the bodies, that is fine. It's also okay if you choose not to. We fully understand. Please feel free to stay as long as you want. You may notice various items in the caskets with the girls. These are things that were very near and dear to them, and we will be burying them with those items.

"The burial service will be at 10 a.m. tomorrow at the cemetery in Monument. You are all, of course, invited. I believe Linnaea has given you all directions.

"At the front of the room here tonight you'll see some notebooks. Feel free to stop by and write a note, tell a story, or whatever. We'd love to have a memory of your coming to be with us."

By the time we left the Shrine of Remembrance that evening, it was about seven o'clock. We talked the limo driver into swinging through the Walgreens pharmacy drive-through (an interesting sight!) so we could collect the medications David needed. Then we headed back to Residence Inn for our first night together as a family in a week and a half.

Linnaea, ever the practical one, headed out to a nearby Outback Steakhouse and a Black-eyed Pea to get carry-out dinners for us. David was hungry by now. Meatloaf and mashed potatoes tasted great to him, a sharp contrast to just 48 hours earlier. In fact, he wolfed down the entire meal. I could tell he was really coming along well, at least physically.

He was a little worried that night about sleeping in an ordinary bed, without handholds, rails, or nearby light switches. But we managed to set up his vacuum machine on the floor nearby, and he actually slept quite well. So did I. We definitely needed the rest in order to face the next day.

"The viewing wasn't as hard as I imagined," David said. "I thought I was going to break down in a mass of tears. But I realized that wasn't them."

"I know," I answered. "It seemed to be harder for everyone else."

"Well, we've had some time to deal with this," he commented. "For others, this is the first time to see the reality."

RESTING PLACE

Wednesday, December 19, dawned cold and windy, although the sun was out. David did not have a proper coat for the day, having lost his when it got cut off back in the church parking lot. Gil, our brother-in-law, offered to loan him his.

The burial service would be a private affair; we had invited only 50 or so people, approximately the same group who had attended the viewing the night before. We had told the locals to meet us at the hotel, and from there we would drive up to the Monument cemetery together. The caskets would already be waiting there in place.

When we (plus Connie Schertel and baby Gloria) came out of the Residence Inn that morning, a policeman was waiting—with a limousine and a Cadillac Escalade SUV from the funeral home! We had no idea such things would be provided. The officer motioned us to get in and follow him. Apparently he intended a full police escort.

Up the interstate we drove in procession, getting off at Exit 158 to turn west and take a side road, the Old Denver Highway, the rest of the way instead of disrupting Monument's commercial area. Along the way, we all again delighted in watching the happy, oblivious baby. In 20 minutes or so, we arrived at the rustic cemetery—the first time David had actually seen it. The girls, we knew, would have felt at home.

The terrain, we saw right away, was too rugged for David's wheelchair, especially with all the snow. Monument sits at an altitude of 7,000-feet, so it collects and retains even more snow than Colorado Springs. The limo driver, however, found a way on the frozen ground to get close to the grave sites, close enough that David and I could walk to our seats under the canopy. I held his arm to steady him as he went, then wrapped him in a blanket to try to conserve his limited body heat.

We saw the same faces from the night before, and some new ones who had just arrived. Several of David's fellow Jefferson-Hemings cousins had made the long trip from the East to be present. We were surprised and grateful.

Pastor Ross led in singing "Amazing Grace," accompanied by Brad Sheasby's guitar. Not many of us joined in—it was too cold. But we resonated with the meaning of the words:

Through many dangers, toils and snares
We have already come;
'Twas grace that brought us safe thus far,
And grace will lead us home.

When Pastor Brady spoke, he told the story of how Job lost all his belongings and all his children. At the end, God restored everything to him in double amounts—except his children. He had seven sons and three daughters in the beginning, and God gave him seven sons and three daughters in the end. "God didn't have to give Job double children," Pastor Brady explained, "because the other seven and three were still alive, in heaven. Job and his wife hadn't lost them. Children, you see, are eternal." He then led in prayer.

"And now, I've been asked to introduce Linda Carr-Kraft from Richmond, Virginia, who has a special presentation to make."

The thoughtful, very Southern woman in a stylish coat, who is a descendant of Jefferson's best friend and brother-in-law, stepped forward holding two pewter cups. My husband immediately recognized them as classic Jefferson cups. "David," she explained more for the crowd's benefit than for his, "as you know, the family graveyard at Monticello is a special site for us all. We have brought you some of its soil to sprinkle over the final resting places of your daughters. For they too are descended from Thomas Jefferson; they belong to us, and we to them."

David stood up, a look of amazement on his face. Their thoughtfulness was almost overwhelming. He turned to the crowd and said, "These are my cousins, and we have walked that Monticello graveyard together. In the tradition of Celtic theology, it is called a 'thin place'— a place where God and heaven are especially close." Turning back to his cousins, he added, "It means the world to me that you would do this."

Laurie and Grace were called up to help their father sprinkle the Virginia dirt across the tops of the two steel burial vaults that contained the pine coffins, while everyone watched respectfully. David made the sign of the cross as he recited, "In the name of the Father, and of the Son, and of the Holy Ghost, amen."

Shay Banks-Young from Columbus, Ohio, another of the Hemings

cousins and the mother of two sons in the ministry, then recited an
original poem titled "Butterflies and Me."

> *Like the caterpillar*
> *I have spent life traveling my path*
> > *lying flat on my stomach*
> *Crawling little by little . . . one step at a time*
> *My face, hands and legs touching always*
> *The soil of the earth.*
> *One day, I found myself facing the tree of life, and*
> *With what strength I had left*
> *I crawled up to the nearest limb and prayed for*
> > *direction and peace.*
> *God heard my prayer . . .*
> *And surrounded me with the cocoon of his love.*
> *The love was so strong, that the effects . . .*
> > *caused me to fall into a great sleep*
> > *only to find*
> *Upon my awakening that I would no longer have to crawl . . .*
> *For I had been given Wings of Eternal Life.*[6]

It was finally time for the lowering of the vaults into the graves,
with the mourners still watching—a tradition in this cemetery. It took
several minutes for the workers to prepare the mechanics of this operation. To fill the time lag, David said to Pastor Ross, "Let us teach you
an old family song of ours. We learned this way back when the girls
were little." He then began to sing.

> *How great is our God, how great is his name;*
> *He's the greatest one, forever the same.*
> *He rolled back the waters of the mighty Red Sea,*

And he says, "I'll never leave you, so put your trust in me."[7]

We sang it several times as a statement of our faith in a God who would not abandon us now. He would lead us through the waters of grief that lay ahead. His nature would remain forever the same. He would be our great tower of strength through the admittedly tough future we faced.

Our final act that morning was to spread flower petals on the lowered vaults. We placed a red rose on the snowy ground at the head of each opening, where the markers would eventually be situated. Roses had always been a romantic favorite in our family, and these two signified the vibrant life of our daughters, even in the dead of winter.

As we rode back to the hotel for a short break before the afternoon memorial, our hearts were full. One more step had been completed in this long walk of trust and endurance. We would never entirely get over the loss of Stephanie and Rachel. But neither would we give in to despair or bitterness. We would keep moving forward in the present moment and keep looking to find the face of God at every turn.

CELEBRATION
OF LIFE

We were a little late entering the sanctuary from the side staging room (normally New Life's youth chapel), so that most of the crowd of 3,000 were already in place. We had hoped the family members could all be seated ahead of the rush, but time slipped away.

Rolling across the foyer in my wheelchair, I (David) was startled to see a long line of news photographers waiting. I hadn't expected this to be such a large media event. I got a further jolt the minute I came through the doorway at the top of the sloping aisle between sections 11 and 12 of the circular auditorium. A sea of faces suddenly turned toward me and my family members, as people stood in silent respect.

Tears began to well up in my eyes. For a fleeting moment, I remembered the counselor's advice that whenever I felt like crying, I should let it come; it would be healthy for me in the grief process. *Well, not now,* I lectured myself. *Hold it together for this very public scene.* I spent most of my journey down the aisle working to compose myself.

Along the way, I saw people from various sectors of our lives. A sizable group from the Granby church had driven down. There were First Data teammates, and not just from Denver; some of the Omaha group had come out to join them. There were even senior executives in the audience that day, including First Data's CEO. I was both surprised and gratified that they had interrupted their schedules to attend.

In another section sat Doug McIntyre and his fellow EMTs, who had worked so hard to try to save lives the week before. (Doug told us later that when word had reached the station late Sunday night about Rachel's passing, he and his partners were crushed. They thought for sure they had rescued her. Doug went through a week of depression afterward, with thoughts of actually quitting emergency work—after a 20-year career. A chaplain helped him sort through his emotions.)

The sanctuary was festooned with Christmas poinsettias all around, plus a large spray of red and white carnations behind the podium. The girls' photo enlargement was in place just below the podium, where Pastor Rob Brendle waited for all to find their seats. It took several minutes for everyone to get situated. Then he welcomed the audience to this special "Celebration of Life," as we had chosen to call it. He read the familiar words of 1 Thessalonians 4:13-14: "We do not want you to be ignorant about those who fall asleep, or to grieve like the rest of men, who have no hope. We believe that Jesus died and rose again and so we believe that God will bring with Jesus those who have fallen asleep in him."

He alluded briefly to the story of Horatio Spafford, the Chicago lawyer whose wife and four daughters were on a ship that collided with another vessel in the mid-Atlantic and sank in 1873. The four girls perished in the icy water. Spafford quickly sailed for England to find his wife. While crossing the ocean, the captain advised him one day that they were at about the same location as the tragedy. He retreated to his stateroom and wrote the words that became a classic hymn:

Stephanie and Laurie wrestling with Dad. Whitefish, Mont.

Rachel and Laurie on Rachel's first birthday.

The Three Musketeers, Laurie, Stephanie and Rachel, at our house in Whitefish, Mont.

Stephanie, Laurie, Grace and Rachel with their stuffed animals in our apartment in Denver.

Laurie, Stephanie, Grace and Rachel at Disney World, Orlando, 2004. We didn't take that many pictures—Splash Mountain and Pirates of the Caribbean were far more important.

Stephanie, Rachel, Laurie and Grace. The three older girls attended Desperation Summer Intensive in 2006 at New Life Church. This was instrumental in our moving to New Life Church later that year.

Rachel with the Holy Cross Wilderness in the background from the top of Vail Mountain, summer 2006. We loved going up to Vail to hike.

Rachel, Stephanie, Laurie and Grace. Labor Day weekend we went to Pikes Peak, Mt. Evans, and then camping near the Indian Peaks Wilderness. While hiking, we came across this creek. The girls set this shot up themselves. It's one of our favorite photos.

Stephanie on a train at the KC Rail Experience,
Union Station, Kansas City.

Stephanie posing at the ruins of a building in Kansas City next
to a theater where her grandmother (David's mom) was leading a
production. One of her "royal" poses, which came to her naturally.

Rachel and Stephanie goofing around on our couch in the Denver apartment. Even though they were opposites in personality, toward the end they were becoming very close friends.

Rachel's best friend, Aimee, came to visit around New Year's 2007. They went to theMILL on Friday night.

Stephanie on her 18th birthday, January 28, 2007.

Stephanie and Rachel showing off their freshly painted
fingernails in Rachel's room, May 2007.

This is Rachel giving her testimony during her Global Expeditions (Teen Mania) missions trip to Mexico, 2007. This is the first time she had ever done so publicly and was very proud of her accomplishment. This was in a garbage dump.

Rachel with a young girl during her Mexico missions trip, 2007.

Stephanie posing on the Great Wall, China, 2007.

All of the girls love taking photographs, especially Rachel.
This was taken in China.

Laurie and Stephanie at the Forbidden City, China, 2007.

Rachel on a swing in China. This is where she found and comforted a young boy who was also homesick.

Stephanie on the beach in Hong Kong. She didn't take her swimsuit because she thought the beach would be gross. However, after she saw how gorgeous it was, she jumped in with all her clothes on.

Stephanie pouring out tea in a Hong Kong restaurant. She was a tea connoisseur.

Our family loves Chinese food, especially egg drop soup. But you always wonder, "Do they really eat this in China, and if they do, does it taste the same?" Rachel is finding out. . . .

On the China missions trip, Rachel was able to fulfill one of her dreams—doing archery. She was a huge fan of Susan in "The Chronicles of Narnia" series and Legolas from "The Lord of the Rings" trilogy.

Stephanie and Rachel on the bus returning to Hong Kong from the beach. It was taken by Rachel and was on her Facebook page. This photo was enlarged and used at the funeral.

Stephanie on the top of Mt. Evans, west of Denver. Labor Day weekend, 2007.

Rachel, Grace, Laurie, David, Marie and Stephanie, January 2006.

Marie's window shot out. Note the window is also shot out on the sliding door. You can see the passenger window has been shattered but is still in place. A bullet went through both passenger and driver head rests. In the parking lot at New Life Church, December 9, 2007.

The shattered door, New Life Church, December 2007.

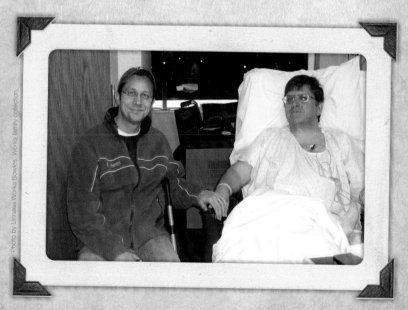

Saturday evening in the hospital. This is Pastor Ross Parsley of
New Life Church. We are good friends and also charter members of
the "It's just not right to shave on Saturday" club. Though I look
mad here, I wasn't. I was just horribly nauseated!

Works family with Pastor Brady Boyd of New Life Church.

Christmas tree and Silver Bells

Spring Petals

Starry Night

These are just a few of the fashion designs Grace produced. This project started from a strong sense that she might become a fashion designer when she grows up, but ended up being a God-given process of bringing hope back into her life.

When peace like a river attendeth my way;
When sorrows like sea billows roll;
Whatever my lot, Thou hast taught me to say,
"It is well, it is well with my soul."

I had no elegant poetry to offer that day, but as I listened, I felt some of the same peace in the wake of our own terrible loss. I took a deep breath as Pastor Rob led in an opening prayer for God to comfort and assure us all.

Then it was my turn to say a few words. By now I had disconnected myself from the battery-powered wound vacuum that I had hidden inside a dark green backpack. I could be away from its suction for a brief period. I walked over to a podium that had been conveniently placed on the floor for me, put on my glasses, and read from my script: "On behalf of my wife, Marie, and my daughters Laurie and Grace, I want to thank you for coming to celebrate the lives of Stephanie and Rachel. I also need to thank a number of people, if you'll indulge me for a moment.

"I need to thank God. In the words of the old spiritual, 'We've come a long way, Lord—a mighty long way.'" I was referring specifically—although many in the crowd wouldn't know—to the weekend slump I had endured physically and psychologically. Back on Sunday afternoon and evening, I had no hope of being here for this service. The idea of my standing up and speaking publicly was preposterous. I felt that the "mighty long way" God had brought me by this Wednesday afternoon was little short of a miracle.

I went on to thank the New Life Church family, my employer, the first-responder agencies, and the staff at Penrose Hospital. I specifically named my sister and my brother, giving appreciation for their kindnesses.

Then I said, in conclusion, "I'd like to share some verses that came several months ago to our family in which we found particular comfort. They seem much more poignant today. I am reading from a framed copy that hung in our grandparents' cabin in Gilpin County." I took time along the way to emphasize particular phrases (rendered here in bold italic type):

The Lord is my shepherd; I shall not want.
He maketh me to lie down in green pastures:
he leadeth me beside the still waters.
He restoreth my soul:
he leadeth me in the paths of righteousness for his name's sake.
Yea, *though I walk through the valley of the shadow of death,*
I will fear no evil: for thou art with me;
thy rod and thy staff they comfort me.
Thou preparest a table before me *in the presence of mine enemies:*
thou anointest my head with oil; my cup runneth over.
Surely goodness and mercy shall follow me all the days of my life:
and I will dwell in the house of the LORD for ever.
—Psalm 23 (KJV)

Each of these phrases carried a distinct impact for our family. I didn't try to elaborate for the audience that day, but the loved ones on the front row knew what I was talking about. And others no doubt figured it out.

IN HIS PRESENCE

Pastor Ross and the musicians then began to lead us in worship. For nearly 15 minutes they focused our attention through a song titled "Here in Your Presence," followed by "The Hiding Place," both written by New Life staff members. Some attendees may not have expected to sing at a funeral, but we found it entirely natural. Marie, in fact, became so engaged that she stood up, lifted baby Gloria into her arms, and began to gently dance while holding her. Though Stephanie might no longer be there to dance before the Lord, her mother could take her place. Marie told me later, "I didn't want to just sit there and listen to the music. I wanted to enter into worship."

When I saw this, I stood up. Soon the audience was on its feet. The sounds of adoration and trust in God filled the building.

The theme continued when Grace and Laurie went up to the microphone (along with Laurie's boyfriend, Jesse, for support). From an open Bible, Grace read Stephanie's favorite Scripture: "You turned my wailing into dancing; you removed my sackcloth and clothed me with joy, that my heart may sing to you and not be silent. O LORD my God, I will give you thanks forever" (Psalm 30:11-12).

Laurie then introduced a favorite of Rachel's—in fact, her last entry in the journal we placed in her casket: Philippians 4:6-7. "Don't worry about anything; instead, pray about everything. Tell God what you need, and thank him for all he has done. If you do this, you will experience God's peace, which is far more wonderful than the human mind can understand. His peace will guard your hearts and minds as you live in Christ Jesus" (NLT).

And then it was back to music again. Jessie Gingrich, who had been within inches of us when the bullets flew back on December 9, sang a powerful duet with Glenn Packiam titled "Everlasting God." Pastor Ross and the team followed up with another audience song, "Everyone Overcome," during which pictures of the girls on mission trips filled the overhead screens. The synergy could not have been more powerful—these young girls taking the light and power of Jesus to far corners of the world, pushing back the darkness. Even in their deaths, we felt they were overcomers.

HEAVEN'S TOUR GUIDES

When everyone sat down again, our former pastor from Granby, Randy Payne, came up to read the girls' obituaries and also tell how warmly they used to greet him on Sunday mornings when they were little, wrapping their arms around his legs. Following this, four young people came to the microphone to share memories:

Connie Schertel spoke about how she and Stephanie kept their friendship going despite the distance between them.

Rachel Villareal, who was on the China trip, highlighted Stephanie's free abandon in worship ("She was a dancing fool before the Lord!") but also said she was "blessed with uncommon wisdom."

Aimee Donahue, Rachel's teammate on the Brazil trip, told about daily phone calls and texting. She said when she got the news of the shooting, she had cried for 13 hours straight, until 6:00 the next morning.

J. T. Weatherford, a young man, spoke about Rachel's ministry on the China team and read Revelation 21:1-5, the Bible's description of the "new heaven."

> Then I saw a new heaven and a new earth, for the first heaven and the first earth had passed away, and there was no longer any sea. I saw the Holy City, the new Jerusalem, coming down out of heaven from God, prepared as a bride beautifully dressed for her husband. And I heard a loud voice from the throne saying, "Now the dwelling of God is with men, and he will live with them. They will be his people, and God himself will be with them and be their God. He will wipe every tear from their eyes. There will be no more death or mourning or crying or pain, for the old order of things has passed away."
>
> He who was seated on the throne said, "I am making every-

thing new!" Then he said, "Write this down, for these words are trustworthy and true."

A short but meaningful video then came up on the screens from an Orlando minister who has meant a great deal to me over the years, Mark Chironna. He expressed both his love for our family and his sorrow over what we were going through.

Then it was time for New Life's senior pastor, Brady Boyd, to give the eulogy. He admitted that, having been at this large church less than four months, he had not gotten to know our girls in depth. But he said that the testimony of others was enough to tell him that they were very special.

He then began to focus on what heaven is like, as described in Revelation 21. He read farther into the chapter than J. T. had gone, picturing for us this massive city in the shape of a cube, 1,500 miles on each side. He talked about the precious stones that adorn the walls, and the never-ending light that pervades everything. Then he made his application:

"It's my guess that Stephanie and Rachel are already busy exploring this place! They've probably already covered a couple of floors and are setting up tours for the rest of us when we get there.

"Heaven, you see, is where you and I are designed to live. It's our intended future. That is why I say to you today: Live life on purpose. Every day here on earth matters, because it affects our outcome at the end of life. Every relationship matters. Every person matters.

"That's the legacy of Stephanie and Rachel Works. They didn't waste time. They lived their lives with the goal of heaven in view."

Near the end of his 15-minute message, he took time for a personal word to us. "David, you're a good dad," he said tenderly. "You did everything you could that day in the parking lot. Marie, you're a good mom. You did everything you could for your girls." I choked up at this as I reached out for Marie's hand. It felt good to have someone acknowledge that although I hadn't been able to reach either girl in those dreadful moments, I had given it my best. And the day would come when I would see their excited faces in a new place, saying, "Okay, Dad, let us show you the coolest things they have here!"

After a closing prayer, we were dismissed. Pastor Brady announced that a video camera was waiting on the concourse outside section 9, where people could stop by and express their wishes and thoughts for us to view later. A large number of attenders took advantage of this.

We left the sanctuary that day with full hearts, heading back to the youth chapel for a reception. By now, I was eager to get out of the wheelchair and just stand, so I could talk eye-to-eye with our relatives and close friends. This went on for a good while, and I was surprised at my growing stamina. By the time we left the church around 5:30, it was already dark outside.

It had been a very long day and we had made it through. My body had held up without the telltale yawn signaling its imminent shutdown. The memorial service, instead of being a sad occasion, had ended up being a worship service. Rather than wearing us down, it had actually renewed our energy.

The support from friends who had come locally and from afar was overwhelming. Ten days before, we had been just ordinary members of New Life who sat in the seats like everyone else, fairly indistinguishable. Now the church family as well as our own families, the community, my coworkers, and our friends had poured out their love and concern for us when we needed it most.

ECHOES FROM AFAR

Further perspectives came our way in the following days from people who were not even at the memorial service. A judge in Michigan named Laura Frawley was on the bench that afternoon dealing with her caseload of drug offenders. She wrote an e-mail the next day that was forwarded to us, describing what had occurred:

> We had Drug Court yesterday. I went in with a heavy heart. You were on my mind, as I knew the memorial service was taking place. As we went through the docket and I listened to each individual—hardcore alcoholics and substance abusers—talk about the pressures they were facing this [Christmas] season and how they planned to cope with it, I thought of you.
>
> When the participants were done speaking, I told them I did understand how difficult the holidays were for many of them. I told them that at that very moment, in Colorado Springs a memorial service was going on for two young women. I told them what had happened to your family. . . . As I was telling them your story, I began to cry. I was upset with myself for crying, but I pressed on.
>
> I told them not to focus on the pressures or the difficulties, but [on] the opportunities. The fact that they each are still here and alive gives them another chance to make a better choice and to change their lives. I told them, "This season, when you are tempted to self-pity, think of Stephanie and Rachel, and make a better choice. You still have the opportunity to say 'I love you' to your families."
>
> When I looked up, the entire courtroom was weeping—even the bailiff. Many people had their arms around each other. I could see from their faces that they knew they had been given the grace to change their lives and love their families. I know many of them will carry Stephanie and Rachel in their hearts over the holidays. The memory of your daughters will help them make the right choices when faced with temptation.
>
> I hope this will be a comfort to you.

We were amazed. We saw this as one of the ways God was turning something evil into something good. Their deaths were having more meaning. They weren't totally random.

Among the cards that began arriving, we found a letter from Connie Schertel's father, Ben, a utility-truck driver in Montana. He had clearly invested much thought in what he wrote. He dared to cast a new light on the death of our girls, calling it a case of bona-fide persecution, in that the shooter was intentionally on the hunt for Christians. Ben advised:

> Go ahead and grieve, and we grieve with you, but if those girls could communicate with us they would gently correct us and remind us to be exceeding glad because they suffered for right-eousness' sake, and great is their reward in heaven. See 1 Peter 4:12-19. . . .
>
> Of course, persecution is not of God. Yet it is sacred as far as the persecuted one is concerned, and sacred in God's eyes. Persecution is the work of the devil, yes, but it is different from other works of the devil such as sin, sickness, etc. We hate sin, but we embrace and accept persecution because Jesus did so, and we are required to follow in his steps. He is our example.

Ben went on to talk about how most people view persecution by an evil regime or dictator in one way but place persecution by a random individual in a different category. They are the same, he argued.

> The death of your girls is no less precious or heroic in the sight of God than the martyrdom of Nate Saint and Jim Elliot [missionaries killed in Ecuador in 1956], or the saints of old who were burned at the stake. If Richard Wurmbrand [Romanian pastor under the Communists] were still here and could read

this, he would say amen. Please be encouraged. Please be up-
lifted in all your grief. Massive opportunity stands before you.
You have the attention of the nation. . . . Be bold. Be strong. . . .
Do not be silent.

Martyrs? We had not yet thought of our girls in this way. They certainly had not been ordained or commissioned as career missionaries.
But the more we reviewed Ben's comments, the more we saw his point.
Our family, by identifying with this prominent church, had unwittingly
put ourselves in the line of fire. We had accepted the mark of those
who loved God. Stephanie and Rachel had paid the ultimate price for
that identification.

Whether this constituted an entrée to address "the nation," as Ben
said, we had no idea. We could barely take care of our own issues for
now. But in our hearts, we were silently proud of our daughters for the
life they had lived and the passion they had carried for Jesus. If that
meant their years being cut short, it was death with honor. It was a
"crown of glory that will never fade away" (1 Peter 5:4). Our personal
loss was an undeniable gain for the kingdom of heaven.

A Christmas
Like No Other

Thursday was heading-home day for many of my (Marie's) relatives. We thanked them for dropping everything in the middle of a busy Christmas season to come be with us. Now they would return to their own holiday events.

The only thing on our personal schedule that day was an interview with ABC's *Good Morning America*. The media had been pushing to get us on camera all along, and Pastor Rob Brendle had done a good job of shielding us throughout the whole hospital period and the memorial observances. He had actually struck a deal with the networks: an exclusive interview with *one* of the morning shows in exchange for all the rest of them leaving us alone! If they would not agree to this, then nobody would get anything.

The journalists agreed. Pastor Rob did his homework and told us he felt the *Good Morning America* proposal, with interviewer Dan Harris, would be best. They had promised "softball questions"—nothing that pried into our still-raw emotions. We said okay.

The interview happened in a side room of the World Prayer Center just across the field from where we were staying. Laurie joined us on-camera, but not Gracie, although she was in the room watching. The entire taping took two hours—for just four minutes and twenty-seven seconds of actual air time the next morning. But we felt good about how it went.

Many of Dan Harris's questions dealt with the details of what we remembered from that Sunday, but we also got to say some important things. He seemed surprised when I said I had no reason to hate Matthew Murray. I based this on the fact that God had forgiven us for our sins, and that our girls were now in heaven, a far better place. "If my girls didn't know God, and I didn't know where they were going after they died, then I probably couldn't forgive," I added.

MOVING DAYS

The next day, Friday, we got serious about preparing to move. I had already seen the patio home just a few miles north of the church that Pastor Justin and Linnaea had networked to find for us. David had only viewed it online. It was wonderful, spacious, and clean. It had a great room on the main floor as well as a kitchen, a master bedroom, and an office for David. Laurie and Grace would each have access to a bedroom downstairs. And yes, it was part of a gated community, just as we had hoped. It felt like a true refuge for us.

So David and I drove to Denver to begin packing ahead of the volunteer moving crew from New Life that would show up on Saturday morning. When we pulled into the apartment complex, we were so relieved that this would no longer be our home. We thought back to all the trials we had experienced there—all the times the girls had gotten bullied back in earlier days by other kids in the area, all the loud parties we had endured. I remembered the college girls who lived above us at one point and how their noise drove us crazy. I had prayed, "God, do I really have to love these girls?" He seemed to answer yes. So I made them a pizza one day and took it up as a gesture of goodwill.

The apartment living, we had to admit, had forged a lot of character in us. It had made us deal with adversity. It had taught us that we didn't always get our way in life. It had prepared us to face the heat, embrace humility, and keep trusting God throughout. We had been called upon to forgive those who neither deserved it nor asked for it. Now we were facing the same with Matthew Murray.

We began taking pictures off the wall and packing up books. Rachel and Laurie's room in particular was plastered with posters. "You guys," Linnaea said, "I'm having a real hard time taking these things down. There is so much history here, isn't there?"

We looked around at the *Pirates of the Caribbean* posters, the pictures of world leaders Stephanie hoped to meet one day, a variety of Rachel's mission-trip pictures—the walls were literally covered with memories from the past and dreams of tomorrow. And there on the floor was Rachel's suitcase—still packed and ready to go visit her friend Aimee.

We sorted out things to be saved versus things to be thrown away. We called 1-800-GOT-JUNK? to come by and pick up our old worn-out couch and several rickety chests of drawers. We looked at the two sets of bunk beds and sadly realized we didn't need them both anymore. One set could be given away.

We spent several hours working through the accumulation of more than 10 years of living in the same place. Then we headed back to Colorado Springs. The drive quickly turned into more than we bargained for. A storm was coming, and we had worked fast in order to beat it. However, heavy snow began to fall. Combined with the Friday afternoon rush hour, it took us three hours to get home instead of the normal one hour. This was the most stress our nerves had endured since David had gotten out of the hospital.

Early the next morning, Linnaea's husband, Gil, took charge of organizing the 30 or so New Life volunteers into three teams. One would deal with the apartment itself, and the other two with each of our storage units. Fortunately, the weather was clear. They headed off to Denver in a convoy of trucks and vans.

"You guys just stay here," Gil said to us. "You don't need to exert yourselves. I've done a lot of moving jobs over the years. You just be ready at the new place when we return with all your stuff."

So that's what we did. In a few hours, trucks began arriving. I positioned myself by the door to give guidance as the boxes and other items were brought in: "Okay, put that one here; put that one over there; that goes downstairs; stick that in the garage; hang that in the front closet." I kept it up for 45 minutes or so, and found myself becoming overwhelmed. I couldn't deal with the rapid fire of questions.

My watchful husband saw I was struggling and volunteered to take over for me. He began playing traffic cop in my place, so I could go sit down. As for the church people, they were absolutely wonderful. They not only carried things in but stopped to set up things that needed reassembly, such as beds and bookshelves. The house began to look halfway organized in record time. Not that there still weren't piles of boxes to unpack. But we would definitely be able to sleep there that night.

Sometime during the afternoon, David said quietly to me, "Boy, this spot over here by the patio door would have been perfect for a Christmas tree, wouldn't it? I was going to go get one later—one with two tops. But I'm running out of energy. Oh, well."

Neither one of us realized that a woman overheard us. She quietly recruited another woman, and the two of them left the premises. An hour later, they were back, lugging a genuine Christmas tree! They had even bought a stand for it, ornaments, and lights. With gleeful looks on their faces they proceeded to set it up.

"You guys!" we exclaimed. "This is way above and beyond! We can't believe you'd go out and do something like this."

"We wanted to!" they replied.

The tree even had two top branches of equal height, ready to receive two metallic stars—one silver, the other gold—side by side. The symbolism was not lost on anyone who viewed the tree. Later that evening, our family decorated it, with Jesse helping out.

"Look, Dad," said Grace, "the stars are leaning over to listen to us and watch us!" I looked up and saw that the stars, because of their weight, were indeed leaning our way.

HOLES UNFILLED

The next morning, December 23, we got up and prepared for church. Living this close, we had no excuse for being late to the 11 o'clock service—but we almost were. The row where we always sat was already occupied when we arrived, so we moved across the aisle to another section.

During the service, Pastor Brady looked our way and welcomed us by name, which triggered a standing ovation. We were a little embarrassed; we just wanted to come and worship that Sunday like anyone else. It felt good to be back in a regular service again.

The only thing that didn't feel good was at the end of the praise-and-worship time, when the children were dismissed to go to their teaching sessions and the youth normally returned to their seats from being up front. This was the moment when our girls had always come back to sit with us. Now, Grace departed as usual for her class with the other fifth-graders—but there was no Stephanie or Rachel coming back to join us. Laurie took her place beside us—the only one.

I didn't say anything to David, nor he to me. We just stood there, then looked at each other, as tears filled our eyes.

At the end of the service, many people came around to greet us. "We're praying for you" was the most common remark, and we believed they truly meant it. Some had gifts they wanted to give us—Christmas candles, special cards, books and gifts with little angels. We could sense the love of this congregation. It felt reassuring.

When we got home around one o'clock, it was now exactly two weeks since the horror in the parking lot. We didn't focus on the past, however; I was too preoccupied with how unprepared we were for Christmas. I hadn't done any shopping or baking. The only traditional food I had on hand was a German *stollen* (fruitcake) David had picked up early in the month at a delicatessen in Denver's Cherry Creek area. We always had that treat on Christmas Eve.

I looked at the colorful Advent calendar we had started back on December 1. It had been such a nice one, too. Not only did you get to open a little door for each day of the season, but when you did, you got a piece of chocolate. The last door that was opened, however, was December 8.

The thought of going out to the mall at that late date and buying presents for two girls rather than four—I just couldn't bring myself to do it. I apologized to Laurie and Grace. They both said, "That's all right, Mom—we'll be okay," and came to give me a hug. I knew we shouldn't deprive Laurie and Grace of a decent Christmas. But I felt paralyzed.

"Hey, girls," David said just then, "how about if I give you some money and you go shopping for each other?" (Whew—good idea.)

"Okay!" they both responded.

"Now, here's the deal," he explained, getting out his wallet. "You're not allowed to buy anything for Mom or me. We don't need anything this year. You are to spend this just on each other." (I didn't know that they had already picked up some lotion and other things to give me.)

They were gone several hours, while David and I worked at settling the house. The next day was more of the same. We went to the Christmas Eve service that night at New Life, where several segments of the aborted *Wonderland* musical were performed. The choreography and singing were outstanding, as was Pastor Brady's conclusion.

At the end of the service, a man we didn't know waited to talk to us. He introduced himself and then said, "I just really felt moved by your story. I haven't come to church in a very long time. I heard about what happened to you, so I came this evening just to give to your memorial fund. I didn't know I was sitting right here in the same row with you. But I've rededicated my life to the Lord here tonight."

"That's wonderful," we said. "Thank you so much for telling us." We drove home thinking that Stephanie and Rachel would be very happy to know the impact of their testimonies on total strangers.

Sitting down together in the great room, the four of us enjoyed our traditional *stollen* and coffee. David couldn't have any caffeine, however; his digestive system was still averse to stimulants. (Citrus was another no-no; hence, no orange juice.) I remember going to sleep that night wondering if Christmas would be a total flop for Laurie and Grace, and I felt badly about that. We really didn't have anything special planned.

THE BIG SURPRISE

The next morning, after we finished opening what gifts there were, we noticed a new envelope hanging on the Christmas tree. The outside read, "From Under the Stairs." I recognized the allusion to Harry Potter's room at his aunt and uncle's home, and I knew we'd just received in the mail our pre-ordered DVDs of the entire set of Harry Potter movies, including the fifth movie, released only a week before. (I was in fact bummed about that because Rachel had been our biggest Harry Potter fan.) But what did this title have to do with anything? Was it referring to the DVDs?

"What's this, Mom?" Gracie asked excitedly.

"I don't know," I replied. I looked David's way. He was trying to conceal a grin, I could tell. *What's going on? What has he done?* I wondered.

Laurie and Gracie and I opened the envelope to find the most amazing letter, composed in the voices of Stephanie and Rachel. It started out:

> *Dear Family,*
> *Sorry we are not there this Christmas. Wasn't exactly our idea either.*
> *We really like the tree. And the new place you are living. Isn't it great*
> *to finally be in Colorado Springs?*

Obviously my husband's creative juices had been flowing over the past 24 hours. The note went on to express on their behalf how much they missed us, and how great heaven was. Then they launched into a sisterly back-and-forth:

Stephanie:	*Anyway I had this idea . . .*
Rachel:	*It was both our ideas, Stephanie.*
Stephanie:	*Whatever. . . . We had this idea. Since everyone has been giving all this money, we worked out this plan.*
Rachel:	*Get to the point, Stephanie.*
Stephanie:	*OK, Rachel. Geesh.*
Rachel:	*So we have been bugging Daddy . . . He really is listening better (but don't tell him that). And, I mean, I really want you guys to watch the Harry Potter movies.*
Stephanie:	*And, I guess iPods are okay, but we came up with something even better.*
Both:	*This is our present to all of you.*

"Dad—what in the world is this all about?" Laurie exclaimed.

I was just as perplexed. "I don't understand," I said to my husband.

"Well . . . maybe you need to check out where the envelope says: *under the stairs*. Get it?" he replied with a laugh.

We went thundering down the steps to the lower level. We pulled open the door—and were shocked to see what awaited us in big boxes. There was a home entertainment system that would enhance our family movie-watching times—plus an iMac computer to serve the aspiring video editors among us who dreamed of YouTube fame.

Despite the sadness of the day, the surprise lightened our moods and we had to laugh. We shrieked about how it would have been just like those two to come up with something like this. We laughed at how Stephanie would have been the one to take charge—and how it was definitely Rachel's idea to go "under the stairs." Now we could watch our favorite movies in all their splendor. Up to now, we'd had a little 19-inch TV with one tinny speaker.

"David, how in the world did you get all this stuff?" I asked.

"I went online Sunday afternoon to BestBuy.com and picked it all out, based on what I had researched in *Consumer Reports*. I placed the order and checked the box for local pickup. Then yesterday, Jesse and I went down to get it. It took us two trips, in fact. We hid it in here when you guys weren't around." He was obviously proud of his trickery.

"You are amazing!" I said. "How did you pay for all this?"

"New Life passed along a gift to me on Sunday and said, 'Go have a Christmas,'" he explained. "I looked at the check and thought, *Wow—what should I do with this? What would be something for the whole family to enjoy?* That's what led me down this trail."

The three of us were stunned. We could hardly wait for the setup to be completed. This would be another way to glue our shattered family back together. Christmas was turning out to be an okay day after all.

RHYTHMS
OF GRACE

The days following Christmas can be dreary for anyone, once the festivities calm down, the twinkly lights go off, and the credit-card bills start arriving. In our particular family, we had even more reasons for a post-holiday slump. The reality of daily life without Stephanie and Rachel felt truly strange. The house was much quieter. Everything from setting the table at mealtime to saying good night at bedtime had to be adjusted. Grace wondered how she would pass the days with only one sister to talk to.

For me (David), there was also the personal ordeal of tending to my wounds. The vacuum machine made me feel like I was being pulled all the time—24/7. The tubing was held in place by plastic tape, to which I gradually realized I was allergic; I had a horrible rash across my stomach. When the tape had to be changed, it was excruciating. In the hospital, they had actually boosted my intravenous painkiller before starting the process.

Now, here at home, the visiting nurse would dope me up with two

Percocets before she began ripping away—and even that wasn't enough. Finally she said, "Okay, this isn't working. Let's ditch the vacuum machine and go back to the old-fashioned way of simply bandaging your wounds until they heal. That will let me use just gauze and normal tape."

After I suffered through the process of switching over, the changes became less painful. They happened every other day. The new trouble, however, was that the oozing fluids were no longer being suctioned out; they simply accumulated in the six-by-nine-inch gauze pads. The first day after a change wasn't bad, but by the second day, the pads were prone to leakage as well as smell. I grew afraid to go out in public for fear of having a mess on my hands in an awkward moment.

One day I was lying on the bed getting my bandages changed when I complained to the home healthcare nurse, "I'm just so tired of these Pampers." That's pretty much what they felt like, and I wanted to get past that stage.

She looked at me with a startled expression. "That's it!" she exclaimed. "That's the answer to our problem!"

"What? What are you talking about?"

"Adult pull-ups! If you wore those on top of the bandages, you wouldn't have to worry about a thing."

I headed straight to Wal-Mart that day for a box of Depends. Not that I needed them for incontinence, but they would hold the pads in place and take care of any leaks. They even had an anti-odor component built in. This proved to be a great solution over the next month or so, until my wounds completely closed up.

IN THE PRESENT MOMENT

On Saturday morning, December 29, I was feeling confident enough to stand in front of a Denver audience and address a monthly meeting called "cityprayer." The leaders had known us in the past, and they had asked us to come and share what we were learning through this tragedy.

I looked out at the crowd of about 350 people that day and spoke from my heart for some 15 minutes. I talked about how God had never left us, even through the horror of the past three weeks. Although we didn't understand everything by any means, we knew that He was still right beside us. In my closing section I referred to a devotional classic from the early 1700s called *Abandonment to Divine Providence* by the French Jesuit Jean-Pierre de Caussade.

"This book was more recently published in a new translation under the title *The Sacrament of the Present Moment*. Those of you familiar with Catholic theology will appreciate the depth of this. To Catholics, God is fully present in the Eucharistic elements. They take it literally when Jesus said, 'This is my blood, and this is my body.' They call it *transubstantiation*.

"Now as Protestants, we may not take it that far. However, Jesus is at least *spiritually* present in the Eucharist, or Communion, or whatever your tradition calls it. If you take that idea of God being present at the Lord's Table and extend it to the rest of our living, then you can appreciate God being fully present in this present moment.

"This is an important idea, for after all, he is the 'I Am.' With God there really is no past or future, because he lives in eternity and has no beginning or ending. He always was, and always will be. Therefore, to him, there is only 'now.'

"And if we see him now, in this present moment, then we can enter into an incredible place of peace and rest. We will realize his coming among us. John 1:14 tells how 'The Word became flesh and made his dwelling among us.' He intends to dwell among us today, too. He is here in the very minutes and seconds of our lives."

This concept had been growing in my mind ever since the Sunday-night-Monday-morning turnaround in the hospital. I was coming to realize that I didn't need to organize everything all the time. I didn't need to try to run every show. God could well take care of that Himself, since He was right here, right now, right in each circumstance.

Instead of trying to play God, I could just relax and play David. I was finding this to be wonderfully conducive to rest and peace. My anxiety levels were definitely lower. God was as present in my daily existence as He was in the midst of the most marvelous church service or personal prayer retreat in the mountains. His presence made each and every moment sacred—which, after all, is the root of the word sacrament.

The words of Jesus in Matthew 11:28-30 mesmerized me, especially as rendered in The Message paraphrase: "Are you tired? Worn out? Burned out on religion? Come to me. Get away with me and you'll recover your life. I'll show you how to take a real rest. Walk with me and work with me—watch how I do it. Learn the unforced rhythms of grace. I won't lay anything heavy or ill-fitting on you. Keep company with me and you'll learn to live freely and lightly."

How much better this was than to grind away in human exertion and self-doubt. To yield to God in the present moment was the key to relief and joy. I was fascinated with the word picture "the unforced rhythms of grace." God's grace did not need to be jammed into any pre-set mold. It would simply roll out in its own rhythm, a thing of beauty and joy.

This phrase, in fact, found its way onto a stone bench we ordered, to be placed between the girls' graves. Marie and I felt it was a perfect description of the way the girls had lived their lives before God. It was also the girls' favorite version of that verse.

To believe that God is here in the present moment does not mean that we "feel" or sense Him all the time. Sometimes our antennae have no awareness that He is nearby. We have to go on faith alone. Regardless of our emotional state, the fact remains that God will lead us on whatever path is ours to travel. He is our Guide and Shepherd. We are safer in His care than we would ever be on our own. We can therefore trust Him with the outcomes of our lives.

LUNCH INVITATION

My serenity was put to the test a few days later, when we received a surprising phone call from Pastor Justin. "Pastor Brady got away for a few days after Christmas just to pray and think about everything that's gone on. He came back saying he felt impressed to call Dr. and Mrs. Murray and invite them down to the church for a visit. He thought they might want to see where their son died, so they can get closure."

"That makes sense," I replied.

"So they're coming this Thursday [January 3]. We'll give them a tour to show them the parking lot, the hallway, and so forth. . . . Now here's the other part: We're going to have them stay for a catered lunch in Pastor Brady's office. What about the idea of you folks coming too?"

"Ooooh, I'd have to think about that!" I said. "I don't know what Marie and the girls would say." In the back of my mind, I was going, *Isn't this a little soon?* I had read in the news that the Murrays had already met with the two victim families from the YWAM shooting, so I had assumed our turn would have to come sometime. But that very week? How would I react? How would my wife and daughters react? We'd just gone through Christmas. We'd just moved. New Year's was coming. We hadn't even caught our breath yet.

"That's fine," Pastor Justin replied. "Take your time and talk it over. Then let me know."

I hung up the phone that day and turned to Marie. "Guess what? New Life is having the Murrays come down for a visit to see where everything happened—kind of to help them process stuff. They're going to stay for lunch. *And Pastor Brady asked if we'd come too!*"

"Wow, so soon?" she asked.

Over the next 24 hours, our family did a lot of talking. Up until now, the shooter had been mostly a faceless abstraction to us, not a real person with a dad and a mom and a married sister and a younger brother home on holiday break from a Christian college. Now we were being asked to face the flesh-and-bone reality of the Murrays—the people who had raised the young man who did this to us. Yes, they were Christians, we had been told. But still—could we handle this? What would we even say?

By now we knew more about Matthew from the media reports. We knew he had been home-schooled—just like our kids!—but had come to hate what he viewed as social isolation. We knew he struggled with ADHD. We knew he had bought massive amounts of ammunition by mail order as far back as September and stacked the boxes up at the foot of his bed. He had told Loretta, his mother, "I'm going hunting this fall." We knew he didn't have a job, but instead spent hours every day on the Internet, posting hateful messages to anti-Christian bulletin boards. Just hours before arriving at New Life—*after* the midnight killings at YWAM, in fact—he had posted on the Internet, "Christian America, this is your Columbine."

Still, we had to remind ourselves that he had not come hunting *specifically for our family*. He didn't know us in the least. We just happened to get in his way. It wasn't as if we had a longstanding feud with Matthew that finally boiled over. We were complete strangers to each other.

In fact, I was the only family member who had even actually seen him for just a couple of fleeting glimpses that afternoon. Neither Marie nor Laurie nor Grace ever laid eyes on him. Did Stephanie see him? We will never know. Rachel probably did not, since her back was turned.

We repeated our belief that forgiveness is standard practice for a Christian; it's not optional. This certainly wasn't the first time in our lives when we had been called upon to forgive, and it wouldn't be the last. We had, in fact, gotten lots of practice over the years. The decision to live a forgiving life had been made long ago. We just had to practice it in this case.

"I think what I feel is not anger or resentment," Marie said at one point, "but rather sadness for Matthew. He was a confused, lost soul. And now his parents must be going through sheer torture."

"Dad, I'm not mad at him," Laurie added. "I never have been. From the minute everything started happening, I forgave him. I knew he wasn't targeting us."

By the next morning, we came to the conclusion that we should accept the lunch invitation. If Pastor Brady thought it was time, then we trusted him with that. And God would be present in that dramatic moment, just as in all the others. He would give us the words to say. We couldn't back away.

I called Pastor Justin. "Okay, we're in," I said. "I'm not sure how this is going to go down. But we'll come."

PARENTS
IN PAIN

By the time we four arrived at Pastor Brady's second-floor office that Thursday morning, he was elsewhere on the campus, giving the Murrays their tour. I (Marie) didn't see them even from a distance, which was just as well, because I still wasn't sure how I would react. I knew I would stay in control—there would of course be no screaming or hair pulling. But would I come across as gracious instead of cold, kind instead of reserved? I was unsure.

We sat waiting quietly. Minutes passed. We made small talk among ourselves. We were all edgy.

Then Pastor Brady stepped in, alone. "They're still finishing up the tour with Pastor Brendle," he explained, "but I wanted to check in with you guys. How's everyone doing this morning?"

"Uh, well . . . we're here at least," my husband said.

"That's good," the pastor responded. "Let's pray together, shall we?"

A *wonderful idea*, I thought to myself. He began to pray that God would be present with us all during the next minutes, that He would calm our anxious thoughts, and that the result of this meeting would be positive. David told me later that it was only during this prayer that he finally got a sense of what he should say at the crucial moment. Up to that point, my normally verbal husband had been at a loss for words. He had no "speech" ready to give. Now he sensed that God wanted him simply to show love to this couple and minister to them, letting them know that everything between our two families was going to be all right.

The prayer ended. Pastor Brady left the room. We resumed our waiting.

Presently his secretary poked her head into the office to say, "They're coming now. They'll be here in just another minute."

The four of us stood up. *Lord, give me grace,* I silently prayed.

THE FATEFUL MOMENT

The door opened. Pastor Brady motioned with his arm, and in walked four people. Ron Murray was a tall, slender man with light-colored hair. He obviously had been crying. His head was down; I could hardly see his eyes.

The same was true of his wife, Loretta. Her shoulders were slightly slumped as she walked forward in her burgundy blazer with dark-colored blouse and pants. She came in behind her husband, a look of pained sorrow in her eyes and a posture of heavy shame. She struggled to hold her head up to greet us as they moved into the room.

Just behind Loretta was her brother-in-law, Philip Abeyta—the family's pastor from Denver—and the Murrays' other son, Christopher. He was a handsome young man, well-dressed and seemingly self-confident. I could hardly imagine him being Matthew's brother.

Ron Murray reached out his hand toward David as he said, "I'm so sorry. I'm so sorry. We feel so terrible about what our son did to your family."

David took his hand and, instead of shaking it, began pulling Ron toward him as he announced, "No, that's not what we're going to do." He stretched out his arms for both Ron and Loretta, while I joined them in a fervent embrace. I felt Laurie's and Grace's arms encircling us too— two families united by a common tragedy. Together we cried. Waves of grief and remorse but also redemption seemed to soak our very hearts and minds for several minutes.

"It's okay," we blubbered through our tears. "We forgive you." We continued to cling to one another while the pastors and others in the room stood respectfully at a distance. Our tearful huddle went on for a long, long time. This was a cleansing we all badly needed. We let the emotions of the past four weeks come flooding out of us onto one another's shoulders. It was a holy moment.

Eventually David regained enough composure to say, "You know, it's tough what we're going through—but really, Marie and I wouldn't want to be walking your path right now. You've got it a lot harder than we do."

"Well, we didn't come expecting forgiveness," Ron Murray replied, "but only to say how sorry we are for the loss of your two precious daughters. Just terribly, terribly sorry. . . ."

"There's a verse in the Bible that just came to me," David contin-ued. "I don't know where it is, but I think it says something like, 'Mercy overshadows judgment.'[8] God's mercy is enough for us all today. It's a lot more important right now than judgment. You don't need to be under any kind of condemnation at all."

More hugs, more tears, more Kleenex.

I looked at this broken mother and felt afresh the pain that every mother feels when her best efforts fall short of producing the child she wanted. I knew I hadn't been a perfect mom myself, and yet Stephanie's and Rachel's lives had turned out to be a blessing. Loretta Murray could only yearn for this kind of fulfillment. I felt so sorry for her in that moment.

Soup, Salad, and a Surprise

At last our huddle broke up, and we smiled at each other for the first time. Ron and Loretta seemed visibly relieved of a huge burden. They now stood a little straighter, and their countenances appeared less grave. They were still tentative and reserved, however.

"How about some lunch?" Pastor Brady offered, gesturing toward his conference table, where food awaited. "We had soup and salad brought in from Biaggi's" (a nearby Italian restaurant). None of us felt all that hungry in this moment, but we moved to form a line and take at least something, since it was past noon by now. We then sat down to eat.

We asked the Murrays where they lived. When we heard their address, we realized we had looked at a house for sale in their very neighborhood a few years back. We also found out we knew some of the same Denver pastors and churches. Conversation moved along smoothly with these people.

At one point, Pastor Brady said to them, "You know, before the memorial service for Stephanie and Rachel, we had a chance to just sit around and remember some of the happy things that occurred in the girls' lives. In the middle of all our sadness, it was good for us to look back on better times. What if you did the same thing? Tell us about Matthew when he was little. Tell us some of the happy things you remember about him."

Stories began to come about Matthew and Chris playing together in the park, about how Matthew won a footrace in first grade by an amazing margin, and about his jigsaw-puzzle abilities. He could do a 2,000-piece puzzle in less than two hours, they said. Sometimes he even did puzzles with the picture side down, in order to make it more challenging. In that moment, we were far removed from analysis and recrimination; we were just parents swapping kid stories together. It was obvious that they had cared a great deal for their son and had poured much into his life.

After a while, Pastor Brady had a new idea to propose that took us totally off guard. "Ron and Loretta," he said, "I was just wondering— would you like to meet Jeanne Assam?" This was the church security guard who had brought Matthew down in the end.

Oh, my goodness—I can't believe he's doing this! I thought to myself. I saw David tense up as well. *How is this going to go?*

"Yes, we would," Ron Murray said calmly. "That would be fine."

Pastor Brady got up and went to the door. Soon, the slender, blond-haired woman entered. We had of course heard her name and seen her picture in news conferences but had not actually met her. We held our breath as we watched.

Jeanne walked across to the Murrays and took their hands in hers. "I am so sorry for having to take down your son," she said in a gentle voice.

"That's okay—we fully understand," Ron replied. "He needed to be stopped. You did the right thing."

How surreal is this! David and I were both thinking. The woman who had pumped bullets into their son was being validated for doing so.

They began to talk about what had occurred there in the hallway on December 9. "I never once thought that I was attacking *Matthew*," Jeanne said. "As I was yelling at him over and over to drop his weapon— I must have screamed it half a dozen times—the only thought in my mind was that I had to confront the Enemy."

"You're right," the Murrays replied. "Matthew wasn't himself that day. He had been taken over by the Evil One."

Eventually, there was a time of prayer for Jeanne, during which both Ron and Loretta, as well as Pastor Brady and Pastor Abeyta, asked God to bless her and give her relief from any second thoughts about her action that day.

We then resumed our earlier conversation. We exchanged phone numbers and e-mail addresses with the Murrays. The meeting lasted nearly two hours, until we had to head to another appointment. We left the church that afternoon feeling relieved as well as enlightened. These were people for whom we could only wish God's healing touch in the future.

The next Sunday morning, Pastor Brady took five minutes or so at the beginning of his sermon to update the New Life congregation on what had taken place. He called it "the greatest testimony of forgiveness and redemption that I've ever seen" and "the highlight of my ministry career." We were humbled to have been a part of it.

A day or two later, the Murrays released a statement to the press in which they described the meeting in detail and then said, "God is good, and our entire experience last Thursday was filled with His loving and healing presence. . . . The depth of our sorrow and our grief is greater than we can possibly describe. But with thanks to God, [to] these remarkable families [including the Johnsons and Crouses, whose young adults died at YWAM] and their pastors and churches, healing and reconciliation have begun. We are committed to finding a way to move forward in the service of the Lord and our community."

The whole experience in Pastor Brady's office turned out to be a lot less emotionally taxing for us than David and I had feared. This was the way God's grace works, we reminded ourselves, when you decide to obey His commandments.

QUESTIONS AND ANSWERS

The appointment we rushed to that Thursday afternoon was certainly a shift of gears for us. In less than half an hour we transported ourselves from the airy New Life Church office suite to a conference room at the Colorado Springs Police headquarters. Fifteen to twenty detectives, all dressed in white shirts and ties, were waiting to debrief us on their investigation. They had worked hard to compile a thick notebook of reports, photos, and other information. They had also struggled to clear their schedules so they could all be present for this meeting.

They sat along three sides of a rectangle of tables with an opening in the center, one side being left vacant for the four of us plus a couple of victims' advocates. We had assumed this meeting would be easier for us than meeting with the Murrays. But the visual impact of all these law-enforcement professionals in one place at one time hit us as soon as we walked in.

David tried to crack a joke to ease the seriousness. "Gee, guys, I was only going five miles over the limit," he said. They chuckled politely.

Soon Lieutenant Mark Smith began the verbal presentation. He reviewed the contents of the notebook. He went over the contact information. We learned more about what the victims-advocacy program could do for us, including funds for such expenses as the girls' headstones and a period of counseling for the rest of us.

When the detective came to his summary paragraph, he said, "We do not plan on charging anybody or seeking any indictments in this crime, because the perpetrator is dead, and so far as we know, he acted alone. We have found no evidence of anyone else who was involved."

We weren't surprised at this conclusion; it synchronized with everything we had heard earlier. What did surprise us was the level of interest, in that all these detectives had shown up this day. It was clear they had all been touched by what had happened. For such a seemingly simple case, a huge amount of effort had gone into the investigation.

Then it was time for us to ask questions.

"Do you have a timeline of where Matthew was from the YWAM thing at midnight until he showed up at New Life?" David wanted to know. "What was he doing all those hours?"

"No, we don't, at least not yet," was the reply. "We're still working on that in conjunction with the Arvada Police Department. But we will tell you unofficially that the cell phone records seem to indicate he was in the Springs for an hour or more before he attacked your family."

"What kind of a rifle did he have?" David asked next. "It was awfully loud—didn't sound like a stock AR-15 to me."

"No, it wasn't. It was a Bushmaster XM-15 that he had modified to put on a larger barrel."

"Was he wearing bulletproof stuff?" No, he wasn't, although his upper body looked that way for all the ammunition he was carrying in his vest.

"Was there a hole in the passenger-side door where I was shot?" David asked. "My doctor thought the bullet had gone through a door or something by the way it broke up into fragments."

The detectives looked at each other and then replied, "No, there are no holes in the metal of your car. Only the glass."

"So then what accounts for the shrapnel I got all through me? Why did the bullet fall apart?"

"Don't know the answer to that, sir."

Whatever the cause, it was fortunate that David was not hit by an intact bullet so close to the femoral artery. He might not have survived.

"Okay, tell us what you know about how the girls were hit. Start with Stephanie." The lengthy explanation that followed corrected our misassumptions about what was the entrance wound and what was the exit. The detective not only spoke but also turned his body to demonstrate the trajectory. For the first time, we got the picture of the single bullet burrowing straight through her vital organs, especially the lungs and heart. Soon we were saying, "Okay, that's enough detail. We don't need more explanation."

The information on Rachel's wounds was equally hard to hear. We were stunned at the brutality of the attack. *How in the world did she even make it out of the parking lot?* we wondered.

We finally exhausted our questions. "Thank you all so much for all the work you have done," David said. "I know this wasn't easy for all of you. On behalf of my family, once again, thank you very much."

Sergeant Jeff Jensen finished the meeting by expressing his sorrow over this incident and directing us to our contact for the future, Detective Richard Gysin. The detectives then slowly filed by us as they left the conference room, each one sharing his or her condolences. More than once we heard "God bless you" or "We're praying for you."

We left the building and drove home in a somber mood. Once inside our house, it seemed like all four of us pretty much crashed. David was no longer his talkative self. Laurie seemed struck with the finality of the shooting. Her sisters were never, ever coming back. Gracie, on the other hand, grew almost hyperactive. She was bouncing off the walls, while the other three of us mainly wanted just to find some private space to be alone with our emotions. I couldn't stop thinking about how the bullets had ripped my daughters apart. By mid-evening, I was physically ill.

We had all pumped so much adrenalin into that day, first with the Murrays, then with the police, that we were exhausted. We went to bed early that night and hoped the next day would be more normal.

SHATTERED WINDOWS, SHATTERED LIVES

Early the next week, we drove up to a Denver auto-auction garage to see our shot-up minivan, now released from police custody. The insurance company had taken possession of it as a consequence of totaling out its value and sending us a check. Still, there were some CDs remaining in the CD changer, plus David and I wanted to see the vehicle one last time. This was, after all, the place where Stephanie died.

The first thing to catch David's eye was the large painted word "BIO" (for *biohazard*) on both side windows, indicating that the vehicle had bloodstains inside. We knew that, of course, but it was still a jolt to see the markings. We walked around the vehicle. All the sounds and emotions of that dreadful day came surging back.

David's window (front right) and my window (front left) were completely missing now, as was Stephanie's (middle left). The already punctured glass had apparently been shaken to bits by the towing process. The lower windshield showed two impact marks where Matthew had tried to shoot us head-on, but the bullets had ricocheted off the slanted glass and up over the roof. The driver-side windshield wiper had been blown away.

In the front seat, David's headrest had been shot straight through from right to left, the same bullet apparently traveling onward to hit mine. The leather was split in various places. Obviously, Matthew had been aiming at my head and David's, but missed.

We then moved around to study the front passenger door, where David still wondered (along with Dr. Fisher) if at least one bullet hadn't come through to strike him. There were no holes at all, just as the police had said the previous Thursday. The fragmentation of the bullet that hit David's groin must have had a different cause. Perhaps it was flawed to begin with.

Behind his seat, the plastic molding on the middle fold-up seat (to which Rachel was headed but never made it) showed bullet impact. The seat cushion had been struck as well.

Soon I was ready to leave. But my husband was still curious to get an accurate picture of what happened where. He knelt in the driver's seat and looked over the back, surveying the chaos. *If I don't do this,* he said to himself, *I'm going to be thinking about it the rest of my life. I have to see the exact spot where Stephanie died.*

The bloodstain on the floor was further to the right than he had assumed. Once his mental picture was settled, he was willing to go. He gathered the left-behind music CDs and then returned to me.

We stood there in the garage looking at this hulk and remembered the good times we had enjoyed—the vacation trips to the Midwest, the Sunday drives up to Granby for church, the laughter and singing. But there was no way we could ever drive it again. It was time to move on.

When we got back home and mentioned to people what we had done, they said things like, "Wow, that must have been hard." Yes, it was difficult—but it was also necessary. We needed to reach our own closure on at least the physical aspects of what had befallen us, just as the Murrays needed to see the church locations.

The emotional and psychological parts, however, were still a work in progress.

BACK TO "NORMAL"?

The holidays were over now. All the dramatic meetings and events had come and gone, it seemed. Our calendar for January was mostly blank. I (David) wouldn't even be going back to work yet, as I waited for my wounds to heal.

The Colorado aspen trees were bare in the dead of winter, and snow fell repeatedly throughout the month. A cold snap started on the 16th that sent thermometers in our neighborhood as low as 10 below zero. Staying indoors, we spent our time trying to rekindle some sense of normal family life, but it was hard without two of our main sparks. The house was quiet—way too quiet.

Marie and I found ourselves expecting too much from Laurie, as if she could light up everybody else's life. "Aren't you going to play chess with Gracie?" we heard ourselves nagging. "Stephanie did every day." When Laurie would head out for an evening with friends, we showed our disappointment. Now there would be only three plates at the dinner table, not even four.

"I know I shouldn't feel this way," Marie confessed to me in private, "but when the front door closes behind her, I get swept up with the sensation that I'm losing her, too. I don't know what to do; I'm beside myself with emptiness and loneliness. My heart aches for Grace, too, and how lonely she must feel when Laurie leaves to go anywhere."

"I know what you mean," I said. "We have to keep reminding ourselves that she truly is 18. Almost 19, in fact."

"Yes, you're right."

Another bump in the road had to do with Stephanie's and Rachel's wardrobes. In the process of moving and sorting, Marie and the girls had come across various items they wanted to put to use. Marie latched on to a pretty silk scarf of Stephanie's that had a mixture of greens and navy blue. Laurie was attracted to several shirts that had belonged to both Stephanie and Rachel. Even 11-year-old Grace, though much smaller, liked a particular skirt of Stephanie's that she could wear, although it would skim the ground. She also liked wearing different scarves and hats. All three of them felt a bond with Stephanie or Rachel when they put these on.

But then things turned sour when Marie began noticing items left lying around, hung across a chair or strewn on the floor. It somehow seemed disrespectful to the departed loved ones. She allowed it to go on until she could find the right setting to address the issue.

One Wednesday evening, which had become our family game night and a time to talk about how each of us were doing, Marie said, "I'd like to ask something of you guys. It's been upsetting to me the way you are handling Stephanie's and Rachel's things, leaving them lying around on the floor and everything."

Both Laurie and Grace seemed to know what she meant. Marie continued, "I'd like for all of us to gather up the things we've been using and put them back in the boxes where they were. Somehow it makes me feel as if we've lost even the memory of who they were, and this, I think, will help to put that back together."

"Yeah, I was already sort of thinking about it anyway, Mom," Laurie replied. "We love you!"

When we began to explore the journals that Stephanie and Rachel had left behind, we found much food for thought. We had not realized, for example, how hard Rachel had taken Gramps's death back in 2004. It had really thrown her into a depression, and we weren't paying attention. No wonder she came out of it wanting to start a refuge for depressed girls in New Zealand. Not only had we missed the depression, but we had also missed her testimony of getting free from it.

There were other signs of distress that we had missed along the way. I said to my wife at one point, "You know, I think I have more empathy for the Murrays now that I see what all *I* didn't know about Rachel's inner thinking. What do any of us parents know for sure?"

Somewhere along the way, Laurie told us about a sobering conversation with Rachel back in November that had centered on a premonition. Our family was headed into something really dark, Rachel had told her sister—a "massive storm." When asked what that might be, Rachel responded that she didn't know for sure, but thought it might have something to do with the communication problem Laurie was having at the moment with me. The two girls decided not to air the subject with us, for obvious reasons.

WISE COUNSEL

All of these issues, small and large, became fodder for our Wednesday afternoon counseling sessions. Pastor Justin Spicer had made contact with an excellent center nearby. I began meeting with one counselor, Marie with another, and the girls with a third—an arrangement that continues to the time of this writing. Once in a while we will come together for a group session as a family.

My appointments have turned out to be not as heavy and traumatic as you might imagine. Yes, we talk about loss and grief. But probably more time goes into the practicalities of how to keep the family together—how to relate to my wife—how to be a better dad. We talk about how expectations need to be adjusted in light of the new reality. We explore how faith in God shores up the ability to cope with everyday challenges.

One of the things the counselor said was that it would do me good to broaden my thoughts in the direction of everyday tasks and interests, rather than just sitting around brooding about the tragedy. With plenty of time on my hands, I decided to tackle the refurbishing of my dad's old classic jukebox. It's a 1946 Wurlitzer 1015 Bubbler that plays 78 rpm records from back in the day. He had it in his home office, and whenever our family came over, he'd give the girls nickels and dimes so they could punch the buttons and call up favorite songs. They loved it.

For an information technology guy like me, this was a curious project. No "software" issues here, for sure! Just "hardware" problems like cracked plastic elements to replace, burned-out lightbulbs, mirrors that had fogged over, and a scratchy needle. I found a company back in the Midwest that could supply some of the parts I needed. When they arrived in the mail, it took some filing and fiddling to get them to fit right, but I managed in the end. I spent probably a couple of hours every day on this, until the machine worked smoothly again.

In a sense, it was therapeutic for me to be back in control of *something*. One of the worst parts of the shooting was that control was totally taken away from me. I couldn't do a thing to alter what Matthew Murray had on his mind. My life, and that of my family members, was completely in his hands. An awful feeling.

Here, the jukebox was subject to my control. I derived a certain fulfillment from being able to make it do what I wanted it to do. I even waxed and polished the casing to the point where it was ready to show off to friends who stopped by our house. Every time I looked at it, it reminded me of my dad. I still remembered the day he had brought it home long ago. Now I was putting some of those happy pieces of my childhood back where they belonged.

COLD TURKEY

Sometime in January, I also decided it was about time to wean myself off the nightly Xanax tablet that helped me get to sleep. I went onto the Web and learned I could get hooked on this stuff if I kept taking it past 90 days. Well, I'd already been using it for more than a month, ever since the hospital stay. A nurse there had told me that when I was ready, I should substitute a couple of extra-strength Tylenols instead as I made the transition.

That's what I did. Out went the Xanax bottle all at once. *Hey, I can handle this*, I told myself confidently.

The next day, Marie and I were driving in my Toyota 4Runner down the interstate toward the south-central part of the city toward the car dealers' avenue; we wanted to shop for something to replace the minivan. She was at the wheel and I was in the passenger seat, since my upper-right leg wound was not yet healed enough for me to push an accelerator or brake.

I started to feel jumpy. My anxiety level was soaring. *What's wrong with me?!* I wondered. The traffic was not heavy at all. Nobody was tailgating us or cutting in front of us. There was no external reason for me to be agitated.

About five minutes later, it dawned on me: I was going through withdrawal. The simple act of sitting in the *passenger seat* of a *high-ride vehicle* was calling up the terror of December 9, and I no longer had the medication inside me to subdue it. I was very glad to get to Motor City Drive and plant my feet on solid ground again.

By the next couple of days, however, I was noticing a definite benefit. Without the Xanax, I could actually wake up at seven in the morning with a clear head. Prior to this, I hadn't felt entirely alert until close to noon. I was far better off without the drugs.

Once we bought Marie a normal sedan, I found I was fine when riding in the passenger seat, because it was lower. Only the combination of right-side seating and being up high would trigger anxiety related to the parking lot. Once I recovered enough to drive, I was fine even behind the wheel of my 4Runner truck.

Drugs or no drugs, however, I've become a more wary person. I find that when I'm in a crowd, I'm constantly checking people's hands. Where are they? Is anybody carrying a backpack? Any suspicious-looking characters around? I want to know.

Even in church, as I stand during the time of praise and worship, I'll turn around once or twice to see who might be behind me. Does anyone look strange? I can't stand in the lobby with my back to the doors. I either stand at an angle or look directly at them. When I come out of church, I instinctively scan the parking lot for anything out of the ordinary. It's just something I have to do.

I described this to my counselor and asked if I was being neurotic. He said, "No, this is normal. Don't feel guilty. If you feel the need to check out your surroundings, go right ahead. Do what you need to do. It's okay." He helped me realize that I wasn't expressing fear of a fresh attack; I just wanted to be in control, to know all the facts.

At this point, the counselors tell us that no one in our family is showing signs of post-traumatic stress disorder (PTSD), a very real concern considering what we have gone through. That is a blessing, which we think is fully due to the amount of care we have received not only from the counselors but also from a host of others: Penrose Hospital, the counselors New Life brought in, our extended family members, the New Life congregation, the community of Colorado Springs, and my understanding employer, First Data.

BIRTHDAY TIME

January 26th—Rachel's birthday—would be on a Saturday this year, while the twins' birthday (the 28th) would be the following Monday. Our tradition throughout the years had been to split the difference and celebrate all three girls on the 27th of January. Now the occasion belonged to Laurie alone.

The counselors had suggested that we make definite plans for that weekend, not just let it happen ad hoc. When a New Life family offered us the use of their mountain timeshare up in Summit County, we decided to go skiing. My doctor even cleared me to try the slopes again—after 20 years! I hadn't been on a pair of skis since my single days, when I had lots of extra time and money. Now our family could ski at Keystone and also go out to dinner at the Swiss Chalet in Vail, where we had enjoyed so many happy times in the past.

"Honey, wouldn't it be fun to learn to ski?" I said to my wife. "And Grace, what would you rather learn—skiing or snowboarding?" I continued. "I'd be a lousy instructor, but we could get you some lessons. You really can do this—I know you can!"

My wife looked at me nervously. "Well, I'll give it a try, I guess." Grace, wanting to be like her big sister, leaned toward the snowboard.

The class Marie took that first morning was not entirely successful. She was one of 10 students, the area was crowded (this being a late-January Saturday), and she couldn't always hear the instructor. She worried about how Grace was getting along, but mostly she felt alone and separated from the rest of us.

By noon, when we met for lunch, she was ready to quit. She kept remembering an old true-story movie from the 1970s, *The Other Side of the Mountain,* in which Jill Kinmont skied over a ridge and was paralyzed. The thought of gaining speed and losing any measure of control added to her fear. I encouraged her to stick with the class a little longer.

Grace, who had been in a different class, wasn't thrilled, either. In fact, she was crying and told Marie she didn't want to snowboard anymore.

"It's all right—I'm having a miserable time too," Marie admitted. "But I told your dad I would try some more. He said he would be coming to see how you were doing. Maybe he could ski alongside you."

"No, I don't want to do this anymore! It's too hard, and my legs hurt!"

"Well, let's just wait until he comes, and you can talk to him," Marie answered.

I had been having the time of my life, attacking blue runs and doing better than I ever thought I would. Laurie was enjoying herself too, snowboarding with her boyfriend, Jesse, and his sister Lisa.

"How about if I go to your afternoon class with you, Gracie?" I said to my daughter. "I'll be there to help you along." This proved to be a successful approach. Before long, she was smiling and staying on her board as she ventured down the bunny hill. I called out encouragement to her as I side-slipped off to the side and out of the way. By the end of the day she was actually riding up a short chairlift and boarding back down.

Marie, on the other hand, said her knees were hurting, and she was no doubt going to get seriously injured before long. I decided it was time for me to rethink the balance between challenging her to take risks and pushing her into disaster. We elected to take Sunday off and just relax.

That evening, we drove over to Vail for our birthday fondue at the Swiss Chalet. I could speak German to the waiter, and he would know what I was saying. This place brought back so many memories. Marie and I had come here on our honeymoon, in fact. We'd been back to celebrate the twins' 11th birthday and Rachel's 9th. Just last May on our 20th anniversary, Marie and I had had that long talk here about the coming of "it."

"Could you give us a table out of the main flow of traffic?" I had requested in making the reservation. That was because I assumed one or more of us would fall apart by the end of the evening. I didn't think I could handle being on display without Stephanie and Rachel, and I knew the others were just as vulnerable.

The meat fondue was excellent, as always, and the cheese fondue was outstanding. Both were firsts for Jesse and his sister. We gave them a thorough orientation to the delights of Swiss cuisine. We also had side dishes of *rösti*—Swiss hash browns. Conversation stayed on an even keel throughout the meal.

We had not brought along fancy presents; in a sense, this whole expedition to the mountains was Laurie's birthday present. But we did have birthday cards for her. Then my sentimental wife brought out another card for Laurie—inscribed from Stephanie and Rachel. We began to choke up.

Marie soon followed this up with a card *for* Stephanie, one with a musical chip inside that played "A Wish Is a Dream Your Heart Makes" from the movie *Cinderella*—one of her favorite fairy-tale songs. A parallel card for Rachel featured a song from *Pirates of the Caribbean*, which she had always loved. By now, the whole table was in tears.

"Wow," Laurie said when she opened her twin's card. "This song— it's perfect. It's so . . . Stephanie. She would have loved it."

We drove back to the condo that evening with a jumble of reflections. Marie and I missed our daughters terribly that night, even as we simultaneously cherished the two daughters we still had. Our lives, like skiing itself, could not be entirely controlled. There were bumps and twists and turns that threatened our equilibrium all along the course. But standing frozen in place wasn't really an option. We had to get down this mountain one way or another. It might not be pretty, but with God's help, we would reach the bottom in one piece.

The next morning, Laurie's two guests headed back down to Colorado Springs. I decided to splurge and sign Marie up for a private lesson. This resulted in some measure of progress, although I wondered if she would ever be able to enjoy the sport enough to make it a family staple. After all, I had my own limitations too, which I found the first time I tried a bump (mogul) run. I simply couldn't keep making the quick turns with my skis the way I used to when I was 25 years old. The run wore me out.

We returned home a few days later without any casts or splints, for which we were relieved. We had tested ourselves both physically and emotionally. We had found out what we could conquer—and what we couldn't. That in itself was a worthwhile lesson.

BACK TO WORK

The next Monday, February 4, I drove myself to Denver and walked into First Data for the first time in eight weeks. People welcomed me warmly. "So good to see you, David! Our thoughts and prayers have been with you and your family." I talked on the phone with Jill, my boss, who was out of town that particular day. Together we charted out projects I could do largely from home. The first was to create an online inventory of all the hundreds of other projects the department was working on. This was an important project but didn't have a screaming deadline attached to it. She wisely determined that I shouldn't be placed under a great deal of pressure here at the beginning.

It was good to be back on the job again, even though I was far from being able to do what I had handled before December 9. At that point

I had been moving into being a main troubleshooter for our team. Now I struggled even to put thoughts together in sequence about some of the more routine things. I hoped my competence would come back in time.

I generally worked Mondays and Thursdays in the office, the other days at home. In the office, people would invariably come over to my cubicle or stop me in the halls to talk, if only to express their own sorrow. I had not realized how deeply our situation had affected my coworkers. Taking the time to let people express themselves or ask questions was therapeutic for them. And I found out I needed it too.

A Platform

for Forgiveness

The word about our lunch meeting with the Murray family had traveled fast, to the point that we were invited to join them on a *Focus
on the Family* radio program. This half-hour daily show is heard on more
than a thousand stations across North America, plus other outlets
worldwide. We had listened to many *Focus on the Family* broadcasts over
the years as well as read such famous parenting books as *Dare to Discipline* and *The Strong-Willed Child*. Back in Montana, our young girls had
devoured Focus's children's radio program, *Adventures in Odyssey*, every
Saturday morning.

In December, Ron Murray had called Dr. James Dobson to ask for
his organization's help in answering media requests. "I trust you people,"
Ron had said. So it was only natural for Dr. Dobson to ask both couples
into the studio for an interview. The first proposal involved us and the
Murrays flying to Southern California for a recording session, where
Dr. Dobson was working on another project.

At first Marie and I said yes—but within a couple of days, I called him back. "Please let us change our minds. We're just not emotionally ready right now to leave home, plow through the crowds at an airport, and all that. We want to do the interview, but . . ."

"I fully understand," Dr. Dobson kindly replied. "This can wait until I get back in town." A date in mid-February was then nailed down.

When the day came, Laurie and Grace came with us to the Focus on the Family headquarters just three miles south of New Life Church. Getting out of our car in the parking lot that afternoon, we spotted the Murrays arriving at the same moment. "Hi there!" we greeted them. "Here we are together again."

We went inside and sat talking in the lobby. This was our first chance to meet Cherise, their married daughter. She and Marie quickly got into a conversation about their common work as home-schooling moms. It felt comfortable to be with these folks once more.

Soon we were ushered up the stairs and into Dr. Dobson's office, with its expansive windows facing Pikes Peak. I had seen plenty of photos of this well-known man, but when I met him, I was surprised at his six-foot-two-inch height. (Of course, five-foot-six-inch people like me feel the contrast of such things.)

"Welcome, everybody," he greeted us. "It's so good to have you here today. Thanks for making time to come."

We sat down briefly as he reviewed what would be happening. "We'll go down to the studio and start the taping," he said. "I expect this will turn out to be a two-day program, given all the ground we have to cover. Of course we'll tape longer than the actual 28 minutes per day; our editors will make it all fit later on."

He then asked, "Do either of you couples have anything special that you want to be sure to say?" It became obvious at this point that the Murrays had done their homework. They listed several points they wanted to share. This was fine with us; after all, they were still something of an unknown quantity to the general public, with plenty of mystery surrounding them, whereas our family's story had already been widely told. This would be Ron and Loretta's chance to redeem their name and show their true hearts.

IN THE STUDIO

The Focus on the Family studio sits below ground level, well insulated from outside noise. Large foam-wrapped microphones hang from adjustable booms over a center table. On one side of the room is a large horizontal window into the engineering bay, where technicians sit at a huge control board. On another wall is a second window for the visitors' gallery; Focus gets a constant flow of tourists, and on recording days these visitors like to sit and watch a program being made.

On this day, however, the gallery was empty. "We decided not to have strangers staring at you for this particular topic," Dr. Dobson sensitively explained. "So we closed the gallery. Today, it will be just us."

We breathed a little sigh of relief, even though in the back of our minds we knew our words would eventually be heard by millions. Still, it was nice to keep the atmosphere manageable for the time being. Even the number of staff members in the studio had been kept to a minimum. James Klopfenstein, a Focus on the Family broadcast engineer and the father of Jesse, was there to sit with Laurie and Grace along one wall.

When all the sound checks had been completed, Dr. Dobson led us in prayer before the interview began. He asked God to be with us through this experience, using what we said to help many listeners. Then he said, "Okay, let's roll," and the taping began.

John Fuller, the co-host, introduced the topic and advised listeners that this day's program would be "only for mature audiences"—a cue for parents to get their young children busy doing something else. Dr. Dobson then introduced the Murrays and us. "This broadcast is historic," he said, ". . . a remarkable moment for the parents of the killer and the parents of the victims to come together in mutual sorrow." The conversation then moved into the facts of what happened on December 9, which took a while to describe.

Ron and Loretta got to fill in important background facts about their son. They told about his struggle growing up with attention-deficit hyperactivity disorder (ADHD), and how after kindergarten and just a few weeks of first grade they knew they would need to home-school him. They described the rejection he felt in the outside world when he couldn't seem to sit still and conform to expectations. They told how, as a 19-year-old, Matthew had actually cried when YWAM decided he should not go on the short-term mission to Bosnia.

"When we look back on Matthew's life," Ron Murray said, "we see that unforgiveness led to his being bitter. Not being able to forgive others—it opens you up to the spirit of Satan. When that occurs, it becomes a power that people cannot control. It controls you. On the other hand, forgiveness leads to peace, joy, and contentment."

He and Loretta confessed how shocked and surprised they were by their son's violent rampage. Ron said the family had never owned guns or used them. They were dumbfounded by Matthew's explosion, they said.

After a while, Dr. Dobson said, "David and Marie, where do you find the love and forgiveness we hear you express to them?"

"Well, it's very simple," I answered. "When you've accepted the Lord as your Savior, it's one of those requirements. I made that decision 23 years ago, so I didn't have to remake it two months ago—of course I was going to forgive. You have to walk in forgiveness. That's not just a matter of duty; over the years you realize that your only other choice is to be bitter. And I refuse to be bitter."

"It's a whole lot easier to talk about it than to do it," Dr. Dobson observed.

"Well," I said, looking at Ron and Loretta with a smile, "if the Murrays were lousy people, this would be more difficult! But even so, it wouldn't change the decision."

"Marie, is that how you feel?" Dr. Dobson then asked.

"I would say it this way," she replied. "Because we are Christians, it's easier to forgive. I know they [Stephanie and Rachel] are in a good place." But then she continued to address the Murray component. "Matthew's parents didn't cause what happened. It was his decision. He was an adult."

Dr. Dobson professed amazement. "Boy, that's 1 Corinthians 13 in action," he said, referring to the Bible's famous chapter on love.

"It's also the old-fashioned Golden Rule," I added. "I want to treat the Murrays the way I would want to be treated."

LOVE WITHOUT LIMITS

Eventually the conversation moved along to our January 3 meeting at the church. Again, it took a while to describe the event—Pastor Brady's initial invitation to the Murrays, their tour of the facility, our first meeting, the long hug, the following conversation over lunch. Dr. Dobson again wanted to know how all this had struck us.

"When I saw them," Marie volunteered, "there was nothing I could do but embrace them. My heart went out to them."

She then went on to put some perspective on the day. "Over the last seven or eight years, I have tried to be a godly neighbor to people in our apartment complex in Denver. We didn't have the nicest of neighbors at times, and it was a choice I made over and over to love my neighbors even when they weren't lovely. That helped me to be able to love [in this situation]."

Dr. Dobson then took time to read the words of Jesus in Matthew 5:43-48:

You have heard that it was said, "Love your neighbor and hate your enemy." But I tell you: Love your enemies and pray for those who persecute you, that you may be sons of your Father in heaven. He causes his sun to rise on the evil and the good, and sends rain on the righteous and the unrighteous. If you love those who love you, what reward will you get? Are not even the tax collectors doing that? And if you greet only your brothers, what are you doing more than others? Do not even pagans do that? Be perfect, therefore, as your heavenly Father is perfect.

"This is not a suggestion of Jesus, is it?" Dr. Dobson added. "It's a commandment."

All this time, Laurie and Grace had been quietly waiting on the sidelines. Now Dr. Dobson called Laurie to a microphone to get her take on forgiveness. She spoke about the very first moments, when the bullets were still flying, before she even saw her sisters fall or reached for her cell phone to call 9-1-1. "I instantly forgave your son," she said, looking directly at Ron and Loretta. "As the shots were ringing out, I thought while sitting in the back of the van, *I forgive whoever's doing this*.

"My only other thought was that I wanted the shots to stop. I knew he wasn't doing it out of anger toward me. And even if he had, it wouldn't have made any difference."

Dr. Dobson asked her a question. "Has the healing begun?"

"Somewhat," Laurie answered honestly. "There is still more to be done."

"Are you angry?" he pursued.

"No. Sometimes I get angry because my sisters are gone. But I'm not angry at your son," she stated with another look toward the Murrays. "When I saw you [on January 3], I instantly felt forgiveness and love toward you. I felt the same thing my parents expressed."

We talked on and on about many things; I started to feel sorry for whoever would have to edit this down into some sense of coherence, because we were all over the map. We actually taped for two hours. In the end, Dr. Dobson closed with a moving prayer:

> Heavenly Father, I want to thank You for these two families and the way they have turned to You in a moment of great tragedy. Other people with weaker faith perhaps would blame You, and would blame themselves. Yet You have helped them to find their peace with You.
>
> I ask You to continue to keep Your great arms around them, to bless them in the days ahead when those remembrances come back, that You would be there on those occasions. Lord, though we cannot see how . . . I pray that good will come out of this [tragedy]. I can't imagine how that could occur. But You said that it does, and we ask You to use it in the lives of others, and in the lives of these two families.

Driving home that day, both Marie and I felt uneasy about how we had expressed ourselves. My usual confidence in media situations had seemed to escape me. We were also sobered by the fresh exposure to the Murrays' pain. "They have an awfully hard road to travel, don't they?" Marie said to me. "Especially Loretta. You can just see how devastated she is."

In about 10 days, however, we were pleasantly surprised when Focus on the Family sent us an advance copy of the edited broadcasts. We listened with amazement at what their editors had been able to assemble. We couldn't believe how well it turned out. Even our voice strength was greater than we had sounded in the *Good Morning America* interview back in December.

We got busy sending e-mails to our family and friends as well as work associates, telling them to listen on February 28 and 29. Everybody seemed eager to hear the programs, except for my mother—it would be just too hard to bear, she felt. I understood what she was saying.

In the days and weeks following the airing, we received a great number of positive comments. People said they appreciated our witness for Christ and the way we were handling ourselves in this trial. We could only smile and give thanks for God's grace that was helping us through.

Focus on the Family received a strong flow of phone calls, e-mail, letters, and requests for Internet downloads as well. Some came from people struggling with forgiveness issues; others had suffered the death of a young person in their own family and were comforted. One high-school teacher called to say she had a student very similar to Matthew Murray's profile, and she wondered how best to reach through to him before something drastic happened. Focus responded with professional resources.

The program even ended up airing overseas in Great Britain, Australia, and New Zealand in late May, then onward to English-speaking countries of southern Africa in late August, as well as many others via shortwave. We were especially gratified to realize that our testimony was being heard in some places around the world where we had long hoped to have an impact.

BOUNDARIES FROM ABOVE

The day before our two-part program started, Focus on the Family aired a taped message by Peter Warren, longtime director of the YWAM base in Arvada, where Matthew had first unleashed his fury. Speaking in a church in Castle Rock, Colorado, he had reviewed the tragic facts of how Matthew showed up there a little after midnight asking to stay overnight, how the hospitality coordinator (Tiffany Johnson) had turned him down at that late hour, and how he had then opened fire. It was not until Monday that Peter Warren found out Matthew had been one of their students back in 2002. The leaders at that time, he clarified, had asked the young man not to go on the field assignment but rather to repeat the three-month lecture phase (a different story from what some media outlets had said; namely, that YWAM had "kicked him out").

Turning to the tragedy of two deaths and two injuries, Warren said:

Why would God allow this? God could have stepped in; He's all-powerful. He told Satan he could not kill Job. . . . God is sovereign over all of history. He can step in—but a lot of times He doesn't. Why?

The bottom line is, I don't know. I don't know if I'll ever know. But I have some ideas to offer. . . .

He declared his trust in a God who is "100 percent good," but he acknowledged what Romans 11 says about his actions:

How unsearchable his judgments,
And his paths beyond tracing out!
Who has known the mind of the Lord?
Or who has been his counselor? (verses 33-34)

An illustration helped shed light on God's nonintervention at times. Warren said that if he and his wife were to leave town for a season on a missionary assignment, they might rent out their Denver house to someone else. The renter would be in charge, and if the Warrens happened to stop by in six months, they could not just go barging into the house independently. They would have to respect the rights they had signed over to the renter.

So it is in daily life, Warren said. God has given each of us a certain degree of control. Not everything we do with that control can be called

"God's will." It certainly wasn't in Matthew's case.

However, there is also the reality that God, even while giving us freedom, puts boundaries on that freedom. He doesn't allow us to go as far into mayhem and chaos as we otherwise might. Warren told about the heavy metal door at the YWAM base, which was notorious for failing to shut tightly, even though it had been adjusted numerous times (most recently by Philip Crouse, one of the two who died). That night, "Matthew put his foot in the door, fired 15 bullets down the hallway—but when he [paused] to reload, his foot slipped, and the door closed. This time, it actually shut and locked!" He stood outside banging to get back in, until a car of YWAM students drove into the parking area, scaring him away.

"Was that door a boundary from God?" Warren asked. "Forty-five to fifty people were at that moment sleeping in the building."

In the closing section, the speaker turned to the need for forgiveness. This is the key to overcoming evil, he insisted. "People say, 'You can't forgive someone who hasn't repented.' Yes, you can! Jesus did it when He hung on the cross: 'Father, forgive them, for they do not know what they are doing' (Luke 23:34).

"By forgiving someone, you relinquish the right to be the judge who exacts payment from the guilty party. You hand over that right to God. In so doing, you find the power to move on."

Moving on was our family's task at hand. We clearly knew that forgiving was a vital part of making that happen. And if our story could help nudge other wounded people in the same direction, so much the better.

Sunshine
and Tears

With the coming of spring, our spirits began to lighten along with the sunnier days and the greening lawns. Our daughter Grace got into a streak of working at her sketch pad. She seemed very intent on whatever it was she was creating.

"What are you drawing?" I (Marie) asked her at last.

"I'm just making up some outfits to wear," she replied. Looking over her shoulder, I saw interesting renditions of women's clothing—formals, sundresses, and some dressy combinations of blouses and matching skirts.

"Wow, those are really great!" I said. "I love the patterns you're putting together."

"I'm thinking I might be a fashion designer when I grow up," she announced with an air of determination.

In the evenings, she would sit cross-legged on the floor next to David's recliner and work away with her colored pencils. The results were gorgeous, as far as I was concerned. I really liked what she was creating.

Eventually, she organized her sketches by season: six outfits for spring, nine for summer, and eight for fall. "But I don't know what to do about winter," she said with a frown. "If I draw something that's supposed to be white, it doesn't show up on the page. I'm having trouble. . . ."

"Well, don't give up altogether," I replied. "They don't necessarily have to have white in them."

Yes, the winter season could be a quandary in more ways than one, our family had learned.

When Grace talked about her other seasonal sketches, she bubbled with enthusiasm. She even gave them names. One that featured puffy short sleeves and a large purple flower with pink petals in the center of the dress was called "Spring Petals." A dark green and silver floor-length dress that flared out at the ankles was called "Christmas Tree & Silver Bells." Another floor-length dress with a dark-blue bodice and a lighter blue skirt that featured embroidery work from just above the knee on down was dubbed "Starry Night."

She eventually got five outfits done for winter, completing the set. It was as if she had now reframed the seasons of her world. I encouraged her to take the collection the next Wednesday and show it to her counselor. They could talk about what this project signified for Grace.

"Okay," she replied. "And I also want to show it to my friends at church."

Whether she becomes an actual fashion designer in adulthood remains to be seen. It was encouraging enough for David and me to see our fifth-grader's creative energy flow again with hope.

MEMORY LANE

Teen Mania, the organization with which Rachel had taken her first mission trip to Brazil, was bringing its high-action "Acquire the Fire" event to the Denver Coliseum the weekend of April 18-19. This Friday-night-and-all-day-Saturday spectacular features Christian bands, bold drama, relevant daytime seminars, and passionate speakers who know how to connect with young people. Both Laurie and Grace were enthused to go, especially since Aimee and Sarah Donahue from Virginia would be there.

Instead of driving our girls back and forth the 60 miles each way, we decided to make a family weekend of it by getting a hotel. That way David and I could drop them off at the event and then have hours to ourselves in the city. The hotel we chose happened to be fairly close to where we had once lived.

The weather that weekend was perfect—temperatures in the high 70s and only a few clouds in the sky. On Saturday morning, we decided to hang out at our favorite coffee shop, getting our usual mocha lattes. While sitting there, I began to reminisce about our 11 years in this city. I recalled spending time in this place with my four girls, laughing at something one of them had just read in their latest library books. It brought a smile to my face and warmed my heart. Being here in this coffee shop made them feel close to me again.

Eventually I said to David, "Why don't we go for a walk along the High Line Canal?"

"Okay," he answered. "We've got all this free time. Maybe it's good for us to remember—to get in touch with the reality of what's happened to us."

That part scared me a little. And yet I thought it might be helpful for me, too. So with nothing else pulling at our time or mental energies, we casually gathered up our things and headed for the canal.

Here the memories began to flow. As we walked, we talked about how this had been a favorite place for family jaunts. We recalled the dreams we had nurtured here with our girls—some fulfilled, others left unfulfilled. We forced ourselves to be honest, knowing that soon we would be working on this book, and the larger world would know our story.

This reflective mood continued through lunch and the afternoon, until it was time for us to pick up the girls for their dinner break. We invited Aimee and Sarah to join us for a quick bite at Panda Express. It was nice to see our two with Rachel's friends, but at the same time, we could tell they were having a hard time being together.

Once we dropped the girls back at the coliseum for their evening session, David and I continued our trip down memory lane. On the way back toward the hotel, he said, "Do you want to go by the apartment?"

"I don't think so," I answered.

But then, as we got closer, I changed my mind. "Okay, let's go see the place once more."

We drove into our old complex. We circled the buildings and finally parked outside our previous unit. All kinds of memories came flooding back—some of them bad, of course, but others that were heart warming.

"I don't know—it's almost like I'm expecting Stephanie and Rachel to walk out that door and come across the grass," David said, staring out the windshield. This was the place where we had spent our last night together as a complete family. So much had happened in the meantime.

"Yes," I answered. "We did a lot of living in this place, didn't we?"

"We certainly did. This is pretty much where they became young women. And then . . . something *really bad* happened."

Both of us sat frozen in our seats. We began to feel a great sadness. This apartment, for all its frustrations and noise and lack of elbow room, was the place of our wholeness. We had been an intact family here. We would never be that way again.

An emotional wave began to roll over me unlike anything I had experienced the past four months. It seemed that the numbness in my soul was breaking up at last. I grieved the loss of the precious girls I had raised in this place. David, I could tell, was feeling the same loss.

We talked about our unusual circumstance following the shooting—how we had never come back to live here. We had never faced an overnight in this apartment with two empty beds. Instead, people had jumped in to help us move as quickly as possible. In so doing, we had been able to sidestep the vacuum of a familiar home now robbed of its personality.

"My counselor said something about 're-grieving,'" David remarked just then. "He said I should be aware that around the five- to eight-month period, the grief can come around again. In fact, it may even be worse than the first time. Something will trigger it, and all of a sudden, you feel awful."

When we finally got back to the hotel, I needed something to pick me up a bit, so I decided to walk to the familiar library in the neighborhood. The girls and I had taken so many trips here for books, movies, and magazines. Circling through those stacks, I started to cry. I so wished I could bring them here one more time.

I then walked to the Wild Oats Market (now a Whole Foods Market) where we had often gone for healthy lunches and groceries. I picked up some bottled water before returning to the hotel. Soon it was time for the Acquire the Fire event to end.

That weekend in Denver indeed put both David and me into a slump that lasted several weeks. We somehow felt our loss more deeply. There would be no going back to being a family of six. We were truly *bereaved*—deprived of our beloved daughters, never to hold them again in this life. We felt that desolation at an incredibly deep level.

THE ACHE INSIDE

That next week was tough for David at work because a new software installation was taking place, with outside team members coming into town. He had to be at his best, since he was responsible for this product.

He couldn't just call in and say he was taking a day off. God somehow gave him the stamina to push through, so that by Thursday night, the system was running smoothly.

Friday morning brought us to a long-scheduled appointment at the YWAM base in Arvada. We and the Murrays were slated to attend a chapel service there. Ron and Loretta had already met with the staff and students earlier to express their sorrow and regret, but we had not yet made contact with all of them.

We arrived for the nine o'clock service. When we entered the meeting room, we were guided to chairs next to Ron and Loretta. We said our hellos. Soon the band began the worship time. Peter Warren, the director, then made introductory comments, after which he brought Ron Murray up to say a few words.

"We're so glad to be here today. This is what we wanted for our son—to be among young people excited to serve the Lord." Ron then went on to express his apologies again and to share his own pain.

When David was introduced to speak, he was very forthright. He admitted, "To be honest with you, I really don't feel like being here today. We're in a low spot that our counselors tell us is normal five to eight months after a tragedy. I just want to sit at home and cry. But I know that Marie and I need to be here, to share in your pain, because you've suffered a great loss the same as we have. We're working through this together, aren't we?

"I have this deep ache inside of me as a father. Perhaps you feel an ache too. Believe it or not, it seems to have intensified in the last week or so. And I'm not trying to fight it off, but just let it be. God in His mercy will bring healing to us all, in His time. He is the One who will carry us in His arms."

David then went on to repeat the comments he had made at the end-of-December prayer meeting: that finding God in the present moment is the key to living.

When the meeting ended, I gave Loretta Murray an arrangement of gardenias I had brought along. She had told me previously that whenever she felt a fresh pang of missing her son, she would use it as a reminder to pray for our family. "Here—I've been wanting to give you this," I said. "I want this to be a reminder, every time you catch the scent, to grieve for Matthew. It's okay, it really is. David and I have so much support from people on the outside, but I'm not sure if you do. I want to do whatever I can to help you through this time too."

"Oh, Marie, thank you so much," she cried. "We'll stay in touch. God bless you." We gave each other a warm hug.

David and I (along with Grace, who had accompanied us) went out to lunch with Peter Warren that day. By the end, I could tell that David was emotionally and physically spent. We had intended to stop on the way home at a couple of stores in the Denver area. He ended up staying in the parked car and falling asleep while I went inside to purchase the items. Soon I was as exhausted as he was. We were relieved to get back home that afternoon and simply crash.

The loss of a child is perhaps the most debilitating thing that can strike a parent. It doesn't matter if it unfolds slowly (from a disease) or in a flash, as happened to us. It doesn't matter if the death is random or self-inflicted. The gaping hole is still there, and it hurts terribly. Sometimes you think you're getting past the ache, only to have it surge back unexpectedly.

These are the times when we have to lean hard upon "the Father of compassion and the God of all comfort, who comforts us in all our troubles, so that we can comfort those in any trouble with the comfort we ourselves have received from God" (2 Corinthians 1:3-4). In that same passage, the apostle Paul says, "On him we have set our hope that he will continue to deliver us, as you help us by your prayers" (verses 10-11). The prayers of God's people served to uphold us during this difficult season of re-grieving. We eventually got on our feet again.

What's the Worst?

As time has moved along, we have come to see that in the grand scheme of things, our tragedy was not the worst that could have happened on December 9. After all, two of us died—but four of us lived. If David had been killed (a very real possibility, had he been just a few inches to the right or left as the bullets flew), I would have been left without a source of income to finish raising our kids alone. What a hard road that would have been for me to walk.

Or we could *all* have died that day. The whole Works family could have been obliterated.

How is it that Judy Purcell and her entire family were not killed? Matthew was firing at their vehicle from point-blank range—much closer than when he shot at us. How in the world did he miss everything but Judy's shoulder?

For that matter, how did he fail to kill anyone inside the church, where his targets were confined into a narrow space? As David said earlier, it was a scene ready-made for a bloodbath. Yet no victims died there.

When we hear accounts of the persecuted church in other parts of the world, we know we here in North America have it easy by comparison. We're not being jailed, we're not being denied access to the courts of justice, we're not being starved. Anyone who wants a definition of "really bad" should reflect on what Christians are enduring right now in parts of Asia, Africa, and the Middle East. In our family, we and the girls read the book *In the Presence of My Enemies* by Gracia Burnham, a missionary wife who, with her husband, was held hostage for over a year (2001-2002) by a radical Muslim group in the jungles of the southern Philippines. She got out alive in the end, but Martin did not. Our trauma, by contrast, was very short and to the point.

Since the burial service, we've gone back to read the biblical story of Job, which Pastor Brady mentioned that day at the cemetery. We lost "only" two daughters; this man and his wife lost three—plus seven sons. They lost their entire offspring. Yet the Scripture quotes Job as saying simply, "May the name of the LORD be praised" (Job 1:21).

Not long before, Pastor Brady preached a message on Jesus' words in John 16:33. "In this world you will have trouble. But take heart! I have overcome the world." Trouble of one kind or another is inevitable in this world. Nobody gets a free pass. Only the degree seems to vary from one setting to another. The important thing to remember is who the Overcomer is. Jesus is the One who enables us to keep getting up to face another day, to do the tasks that lie before us here in the present moment, and to avoid the traps of bitterness and self-pity. He is our Source of enduring grace.

I am not saying that what has befallen our family is trivial. We didn't want to play this role, obviously. David and I are now members of a club that no one wants to join. We still mourn the loss of Stephanie and Rachel. Yet we know that we will see them again, and in the meantime, we will go on living here on earth in the strength and peace that God provides. That is greater than the worst trial that could ever come our way.

WHAT WE KNOW—
AND DON'T KNOW

You're probably wondering by now whatever happened to our vision of being a missionary family with a worldwide impact. Was that all just a pipe dream, a self-concocted fantasy? Were we living under a delusion all those years? Or was it something real—but the powers of evil torpedoed it on December 9?

We continue to believe that God genuinely spoke to us, starting back with my (David's) initial vision in May 1985. Neither one of us is willing to call that a hoax. Throughout the years of our marriage, we believe that God has confirmed His intent to use us on a broad scale. In our view, this has been a legitimate word from heaven.

But how it is meant to unfold and what shape it takes—we're not so sure as we once were. Maybe our interpretation of what God had in mind for us—the "it"—was off base. Maybe what we thought God had said to us was different from what He actually meant. We're willing to say we were wrong in the past.

We thought we knew the hows and wheres. We filled our daughters' imaginations with pictures of what the Works family was going to accomplish around the world. Now in the wake of December 9, we don't feel so compelled to drive the implementation of this calling. We don't have to get on the next plane to Bangkok or Nairobi. A peace has settled in. We're willing to wait for God to explain Himself in His time. We'll let Him bring "it" to us, whatever "it" is supposed to be. In the words of Proverbs 16:9, "We can make our plans, but the LORD determines our steps" (NLT).

A crucial part of what I heard back in 1985 was not to put God in a box, but to give Him everything. On December 9, we gave more than we ever imagined we would have to give. The shooting took care of many "boxes" in which we had placed God.

Friends have tried to bolster us in recent months by pointing out that the Good Morning America interview and the Focus on the Family program have already spread far and wide. Perhaps this book will do the same. Are these some of the pieces of what God foretold for our family? Perhaps. But again, we are no longer in the business of declaring fulfillments. We're not going to say we know things that, in fact, we don't. No more God-in-a-box. We are content to let God sort it out.

For the moment, we are immensely grateful to be established and integrated into a good church, enjoying the first home we've ever owned, and receiving the blessing of stable employment. Laurie and Grace both continue to do well, delighting our lives. We're at peace. We're experiencing God in the present moment.

Of course, we still want to make a difference in the world. But what God intends to do with us over the next five, ten, or twenty years is beyond our horizon for now. And we're not worried about it. We have stopped pining and fussing about it. Instead, we are resting in the knowledge that God knows what He's up to, and He will reveal His further strategies in due time. After 20-plus years of being anxious, it feels good just to sit in our living room and gaze out at Pikes Peak in the distance, resting completely in the Lord. We will wait on His schedule.

WHAT'S NOT IN GOD'S PLAN FOR US

While we may be tentative about the specifics of God's will for our family, we can be definite about some things that are *not* included. Here are three things we know for sure that God does not want for us:

To be bitter. Both Marie and I have some experience with bitterness. We came into adulthood disillusioned with organized Christianity. We were turned off by the politics, the inconsistencies, the pompous words and actions of leaders. Why couldn't people just simply follow Christ? Why did we have to put up with all this other baggage? This is much of what pushed us in the direction of house churches for so many years.

At the time, I wouldn't have called my attitude "being bitter"; I would have said I was "being *right*." I thought I was advocating something valuable that other Christians were messing up, and it irked me. The truth is, I was majoring on some definite minors.

Bitterness is what led Matthew Murray over the edge. He, too, had his bones to pick with the church, with the home-schooling concept, with YWAM, with Ted Haggard. These things festered in his soul. He ultimately chose to settle the score in a frightfully violent way.

If I wound up bitter at what he did to our family, wouldn't I be perpetuating another cycle of the same poison?

Once in a while, Pastor Brady will say something on Sunday morning that I don't entirely agree with. So what? Who said I was the ultimate authority on all matters of doctrine and biblical interpretation? Life is too short to get tied up in knots over every little (or big) thing we happen not to appreciate. Part of the Christian walk is learning to rise above bitterness.

To fix blame. This is closely related to the previous point. It's tempting for anyone to point an accusing finger, as in:

"Well, the parents obviously didn't do a very good job of raising that young man."

Or, "The church youth programs missed the warning signals on Matthew back when he was a teenager."

Or, "YWAM didn't handle him right in that training program; they shouldn't have broken his heart over that trip, which is what set him off."

Or, "The gun dealers shouldn't be allowed to sell assault rifles to a guy like this."

Or, "New Life Church should have had a better security system to protect innocent people on their campus."

Or, as a nurse quietly said to me while I sat waiting in my chair that Tuesday morning to check out of the hospital, "Aren't you mad at God?"

I looked at her blankly and then replied, "No, I never even thought about it. God didn't do this. He's not that kind of God at all." There was no point being upset with the One who was *helping* me through this awful trial.

To blame God is to imply that He has all His creatures (including Matthew Murray) on puppet strings, and He can jerk our arm back if He sees us start to do something stupid or wrong. The theory would be that God didn't pull Matthew's strings quickly enough that Sunday afternoon. Surely that isn't an accurate view of the cosmos. Surely we don't want to live in a world where all questionable deeds get a split-second veto from above.

If anything, we might wonder whether God has given His creatures *too much* freedom! We enjoy a very long leash, it seems. That's the way God chose to set up our world, in order that we might freely choose to love and serve Him. When we don't, bad things result.

God was not caught by surprise on December 9. He wasn't sitting there on His throne going, "Oh no! The Works family just got shot up!"

He saw the carnage in that snowy parking lot as one more case of a human being misusing his God-given latitude. I believe it made God incredibly sad. I also believe He immediately went to work helping people, from EMTs to surgeons to pastors to ordinary friends, as they stepped in to soften the damage in ways large and small.

Blame God? No way. Blame the parents, the church, or any other suspects? It's a dead-end street.

To be consumed with "what if?" and "if only" and "why?" It is a nagging temptation, I admit. I already mentioned how in the hospital I wondered if, during those first critical seconds, I could have defended my family somehow. Marie has since reflected along the lines of "What if I had been spending more time in prayer the weeks before? Could God have told me ahead of time to beware?"

The truth is, if either she or I had gotten any such warning, it would have paralyzed us. We wouldn't have left the house for days. We wouldn't have let the four girls out the front door. We would have turned completely paranoid.

This is not in any way to diminish the value of waiting before the Lord and listening for His voice. But He's God—and we're not. He decides what to reveal and what to conceal. We have to trust His judgment in such matters.

Why did only two victims on the whole sprawling New Life Church campus die—and both of them from the same family? Why did everybody else's family get off the hook, so to speak? Marie and I have no idea. And we're not going to stew about it. We do know that our girls were willing to sacrifice all for the cause of Christ. They had laid down their lives a long time before. The fact that they had such a willingness at the ages of 18 and 16 is unusual, yes—but not unjust. The early apostles left one courtroom, where they had been viciously beaten, "rejoicing because they had been counted worthy of suffering disgrace for the Name" (Acts 5:41). The apostle Paul wrote to his fellow Christians,

"We who are alive are always being given over to death for Jesus' sake, so that his life may be revealed in our mortal body" (2 Corinthians 4:11). Paul was eventually killed, history tells us, by a method every bit as bloody and brutal as what our girls suffered.

Nobody today says, "If only Paul had stayed out of sight and avoided arrest, he wouldn't have ended up facing Caesar's executioner." In like manner, we are not going to say, "If only we hadn't taken our girls to church that morning." That kind of thinking isn't productive—and it certainly won't bring our girls back. We choose to focus our thoughts instead on the goodness and wisdom of a God who knows what He's doing as well as allowing. Any second-guessing on our part is pointless.

SIN AND GRACE

Our story might be considered a microcosm of the grand story of humanity's fall and redemption. Romans 5:20 boils it down to a memorable phrase: "Where sin increased, grace increased all the more." It is talking about the rebellion that started in the Garden of Eden and was eventually superseded by the sacrifice of Jesus.

In the parking lot that afternoon, a great sin "increased." But since then, we have seen incredible grace. God has steadied our emotions, He has encouraged us through the loving care of His people, and He has brought many nonbelievers to consider His offer of forgiveness for perhaps the first time in their lives. In fact, we will never know the complete tally of those impacted for good through our daughters' deaths.

We see that same grace in our interior lives as we move along from day to day. We're not consistently strong by any means, but at least (to use a phrase I hear myself repeating often) "we can handle it." In other words, we're getting through, thanks to the grace of God.

I find myself with a new confidence. I'm no longer afraid of a gun pointed at me, for example. Been there, done that. (Not that I'd want to repeat the experience, for sure! But you get my point.) You'd have to find something else to spook me now.

The experience of going through this trauma—not always with the greatest measure of faith or diplomacy, but at least getting through it—has built into our family a certain composure for facing whatever else the future might bring our way. God has proven Himself to be our Rock, our Strong Tower, as the Psalms call Him. Thanks to His stability, we can handle it.

During my college years and soon after, I did some skiing at St. Moritz, the famous Swiss resort. It has a skeleton toboggan run called the Cresta Run—a steep gully that plunges 514 vertical feet with 10 absolutely wicked corners over a distance of three-quarters of a mile. Sleds with headfirst riders can fly up to 88 miles per hour by the time they reach the picturesque village of Celerina at the bottom.

I tried it five times back in 1985 and was immediately hooked. I still keep my pictures on the wall in my home office. I follow the results of the major races via their Web site. I still remember a TV interview with one British winner.

"So how do you do it? What's your secret for success on the Cresta?"

"Well, I get 'round" was all the guy would say. He was referring specifically to the turns on the course. He was saying that he just negotiated the bends, one at a time. Maybe not by much. Maybe not with the greatest style. But enough to stay in the groove and keep the top side up.

That's how Marie and I feel these days. We're getting 'round. We may not look the best in the process. We may not be clocking a world-record time. But God is helping us get down the twisting, turning course of events—and headfirst, no less. Life does go on.

HERE AND NOW . . . THEN AND THERE

We are finding that it is healthiest if we concentrate on the individual day right in front of us. In earlier years, we spent too much energy living for the future. We couldn't wait to see the unfolding of our larger mission. The future was going to be so much better than where we were at the moment, we told ourselves.

Now we're moved to live in the present. This is where God is—right here, right now. This is where He intends to pour out His grace. This is the day that counts. "Tomorrow," as Jesus once said, "will worry about itself" (Matthew 6:34).

When the phone rang back in early January and the voice on the other end asked us to come to a lunch meeting with the Murrays, we gulped—and then told ourselves, "Okay, this is apparently what God is asking of us *today*. We thought it would happen later. But we need to recognize God's leading in the present moment."

Living in the future is called, in our particular church culture, "being prophetic." Some days I think I feel more *pathetic* than "prophetic." All I need to do is manage *today*, be a caring husband *today*, be a good dad *today*, be a productive systems administrator *today*. This is where God intends to use me and bless me as His servant. He wants me to be content here.

I still deal with anxiety at times, I admit. I wouldn't necessarily term it post-traumatic stress; it's just the sensation that life is getting too busy, too jammed, and I can't juggle all the decisions that are calling for my attention at once. I'm learning to say, "Okay, I've had enough for now. Stop. I don't have to make all these decisions immediately." If it ends up costing me a little more money, so be it.

When my chest and diaphragm tighten up, I can still hear Cheri the nurse saying into my ear, "Breathe, David, breathe! In through the nose, out through the mouth!" I need to settle down, clear my brain, and get back in sync with the God of the present moment. This, I know, is the healthy way to live.

The day will come—that eternal day—when we will all stand before God in heaven, and the senseless acts of this world will finally make sense. The big picture will flow across the jumbo screen, and we'll be going, "Oh! So *that* was the point of what happened! *That's* how all the pieces fit together. That is what God was thinking throughout the various episodes of my life. Now I get it!"

In fact, if we could somehow talk to Stephanie and Rachel right now, I wouldn't be surprised to hear them say, "Oh, Dad, here's what this was all about. This meant such-and-such, and that was for the purpose of such-and-such." They would no doubt both be talking at once, clueing in their slightly slow father on the long view of their unexpected departure. They would be excited to have played a role in the drama of the ages.

Our faith tells us that when God sent His child, Jesus, into the world, He too suffered a violent death while still at a young age. It made no sense to those standing around His cross. It was the work of hate-filled men. And yet, was it part of the larger plan of God? Absolutely. It served a grander purpose that ripples all the way to our day.

This is not to imply that Stephanie and Rachel were in any sense messianic. They were common teenagers who loved God like many thousands of others. But we can well envision God using their tragic deaths to advance His greater purposes in the world. Marie and I think we've already seen bits and pieces of that in the stories we've heard of lives touched for good. As the apostle Paul wrote, "Now we see but a poor reflection as in a mirror; then we shall see face to face. Now I know in part; then I shall know fully, even as I am fully known" (1 Corinthians 13:12).

We expect to find out much more when we join our daughters on the Other Side.

Afterword
By Brady Boyd

Our lives were forever changed on December 9, 2007, when Stephanie and Rachel Works were suddenly and tragically taken from us. We felt like life had been taken from all of us. It buckled us to our knees. But there on our knees, we discovered that God was with us. In fact, He had never left us. What we lost can never be replaced. What we learned is eternally priceless.

There are some who believe that once a person becomes a believer in Christ, life becomes a perpetual Disney experience. Scripture never guarantees a life without trouble. Notice some of the final words of Jesus to His disciples: "I have told you these things, so that in me you may have peace. In this world *you will have* trouble. But take heart! I have overcome the world" (John 16:33, emphasis added).

These words proved to be true in the days and weeks following the tragedy at New Life. We had to cling to the truth of this Scripture. We had to take heart because our hearts were hurting and all seemed lost. Trouble is something that attacks you from the outside. The ultimate goal of our Enemy is not just the death of our living bodies, but to destroy the peace that rules our hearts. Satan has no replica for peace. A person whose heart is controlled by God's peace cannot be shaken and cannot be defeated. This is why Satan wants to rob us of peace. This is why Jesus said to guard our hearts and to receive His peace.

It was this peace, this wonderful peace, that settled over the Works family. They grieved. They cried. Their hearts were heavy. But as their pastor, I watched them closely week after week. The peace from heaven was never stolen; it was always there.

Our church never lost its peace either. We gathered three days after the shooting for what we called a family meeting. We needed to be together, to hug, to cry, to grieve. National, state, and local officials as well as pastors and friends from around the country came that Wednesday night to offer their support and encouragement. What happened next was completely unscripted and unplanned. Instead of hopeless despair, our people decided with a holy defiance that their peace would not be stolen. As our worship team, led by Ross Parsley, began to play the song "Everyone Overcome," the room, packed with thousands of people, erupted in worship as pure as any I have ever experienced. It is something I will never forget.

How did so many good things happen as a result of a tragedy? I believe that a crisis reveals your core beliefs. In fact, faith that is never tested can never be trusted. Our faith was tested and it proved trustworthy. A crisis will force people to live what they really believe. This is why a family usually has one of two outcomes when a crisis strikes: They will bond together and in the end be stronger than ever, or they will implode under the pressure of the moment. Both the Works family and the New Life family discovered in the midst of the crisis that what we believed about God and His goodness was true. It had been tested in the fire and could now be trusted more than ever.

I also believe that a crisis is an opportunity to reveal God to the world. I love this passage in Psalm 31: "How great is the goodness you have stored up for those who fear you. You lavish it on those who come to you for protection, blessing them before the watching world" (verse 19, NLT).

The world was watching and Jesus was on display. Satan has never had a plan to destroy God's work on the earth that has succeeded. A drowning Moses ended up in Pharaoh's house to get the world's best leadership training. Joseph the slave ended up as Joseph the ruler of Egypt. The crucified Christ ended up as the resurrected Lord. The

Works family and New Life Church will end up with a greater platform to influence the world for Jesus. I am convinced there are two times that people really watch us: when we are really successful and when we are really tested. David and Marie Works passed the test when everyone was watching, and so did New Life Church.

My prayer for everyone who has read this book is simple. Please know that in your darkest hour, in your most difficult place, during a time when evil seems to be everywhere, God is near. He has never once taken His eyes off you. There has never been one second that God has not seen you or heard you. I know this to be true because it was tested severely in December 2007, and God passed the test.

—BRADY BOYD
Senior Pastor, New Life Church
Colorado Springs, Colorado

Appendix

Cycles of Violence

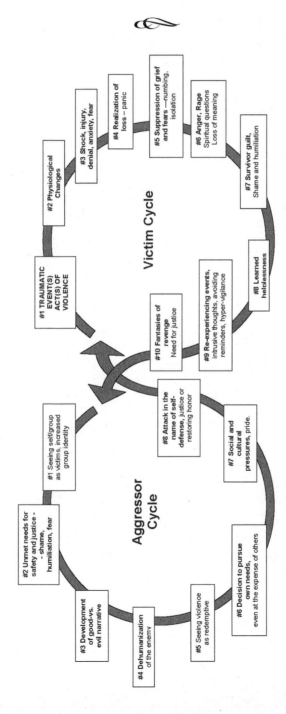

Victim Cycle

#1 TRAUMATIC EVENT(S) ACT(S) OF VIOLENCE

#2 Physiological Changes

#3 Shock, injury, denial, anxiety, fear

#4 Realization of loss — panic

#5 Suppression of grief and fears —numbing, isolation

#6 Anger, Rage Spiritual questions Loss of meaning

#7 Survivor guilt, Shame and humiliation

#8 Learned helplessness

#9 Re-experiencing events, intrusive thoughts, avoiding reminders, hyper-vigilance

#10 Fantasies of revenge Need for justice

Aggressor Cycle

#1 Seeing self/group as victims, increased group identity

#2 Unmet needs for safety and justice - shame, humiliation, fear

#3 Development of good-vs. evil narrative

#4 Dehumanization of the enemy

#5 Seeing violence as redemptive

#6 Decision to pursue own needs, even at the expense of others

#7 Social and cultural pressures, pride.

#8 Attack in the name of self-defense, justice or restoring honor

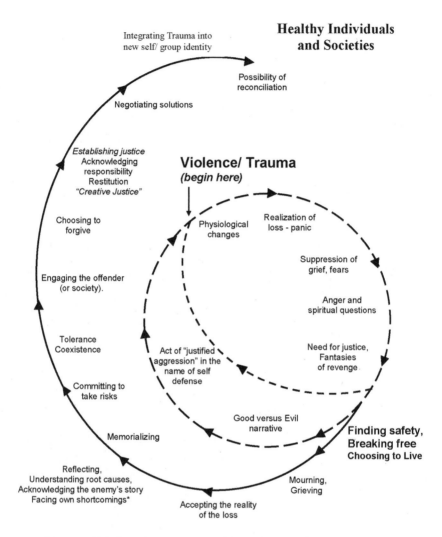

Integrating Trauma into
new self/ group identity

**Healthy Individuals
and Societies**

Possibility of
reconciliation

Negotiating solutions

Establishing justice
Acknowledging
responsibility
Restitution
"Creative Justice"

Violence/ Trauma
(begin here)

Choosing to
forgive

Physiological
changes

Realization of
loss - panic

Suppression of
grief, fears

Anger and
spiritual questions

Engaging the offender
(or society).

Tolerance
Coexistence

Need for justice,
Fantasies
of revenge

Committing to
take risks

Act of "justified
aggression" in the
name of self
defense

Memorializing

Good versus Evil
narrative

**Finding safety,
Breaking free**
Choosing to Live

Reflecting,
Understanding root causes,
Acknowledging the enemy's story
Facing own shortcomings*

Mourning,
Grieving

Accepting the reality
of the loss

Trauma Healing Journey: Breaking Cycles of Violence
*This does not apply in all cases, for example, child sexual abuse

Notes

1. http://www.tatteredcover.com/NASApp/store/IndexJsp?s=local authors&page=303102.
2. Joshua Harris, *I Kissed Dating Goodbye* (Sisters, OR: Multnomah, 1997, 2003).
3. Jon Egan, "Who Are You," © 2006, Vertical Music.
4. A young man scheduled to go on Rachel's Teen Mania missions trip to Mexico back in June 2007—until he collapsed in the training center cafeteria on departure day and died on the spot (from a pre-existing condition). He was at the table right behind Rachel and her friend Aimee. She saw the whole thing—the caved-in chest, his last breath—and felt she never fully processed her grief.
5. Jared Anderson, "I'm Coming Your Way," © 2006, Vertical Worship Songs/ASCAP.
6. Reprinted with permission of the author.
7. Eventually copyrighted in 2002 by Twin Sisters IP, LLC. Words and music by Hal Wright, Karen Mitzo Hilderbrand, and Kim Mitzo Thompson.
8. Actually, the verbatim wording of James 2:12-13 is, "Speak and act as those who are going to be judged by the law that gives freedom, because judgment without mercy will be shown to anyone who has not been merciful. Mercy triumphs over judgment!"

More Great Resources
from Focus on the Family®

When Your Family's Lost a Loved One
Finding Hope Together
by David and Nancy Guthrie
The reminders are everywhere when your family has lost a loved one: an empty chair, a silent crib, an unused pillow. The journey may not be short or smooth, but David and Nancy Guthrie have traveled it—more than once. With empathy and honesty, they'll guide you through the challenges of keeping your family together and strong.

Into the Deep
One Man's Story of How Tragedy Took His Family but Could Not Take His Faith
by Robert Rogers
After the loss of his entire family in a tragic flood, Robert Rogers had every reason to doubt his future and hope. *Into the Deep* is the compelling story of how his faith took root and blossomed through trials, blessings, and a deepening trust in God.

Small Town, Big Miracle
How Love Came to the Least of These
by Bishop W. C. Martin
Possum Trot, an East Texas town so small it's not on most maps, hardly sets the stage for big miracles. But when a local pastor and his wife adopt two children, something amazing happens . . . their church follows in their footsteps! Who would have thought that God would inspire this small-town community to take in 72 of the foster system's most troubled kids? You'll be moved and inspired by this heartwarming tale of modern-day miracles.